Singing the City

LAURIE GRAHAM

Singing the City

The bonds of home in an

industrial landscape

University of Pittsburgh Press

Published by the University of Pittsburgh Press,
Pittsburgh, Pa. 15261
Copyright © 1998, Laurie Graham
All rights reserved
Manufactured in the United States of America
Printed on acid-free paper
10 9 8 7 6 5 4 3 2 1

Library of Congress Cataloging-in-Publication Data

Graham, Laurie.

Singing the city : the bonds of home in an industrial landscape
/ Laurie Graham.

p.   cm.

Includes bibliographic references (p.   ) and index.

ISBN 0-8229-4076-0 (acid-free paper)

1. Pittsburgh (Pa.)—History. 2. Pittsburgh (Pa.)—Social life
and customs. 3. Steel industry and trade—Pennsylvania—
Pittsburgh—History. 4. Graham, Laurie—Homes and haunts—
Pennsylvania—Pittsburgh.   I. Title.

F159.P657 G73 1998

974.8'86—ddc21   98-19735

A CIP catalog record for this book is available from the
British Library.

"When I was a small boy I thought all rivers were yellow and all nights had yellow lights. It was a peculiar drama, and it all seemed very reasonable. I knew that when the sky was not yellow at night, my dad was not working and it was bad. When we went to Indiana to visit relatives, I felt sorry for those children. Their nights were only black and without magic."

— DUANE MICHALS, *I Remember Pittsburgh*

Contents

Singing the City

August 24, 1995. *5:40* A.M. I pull out of the garage and head down the hill past the lights and dark forms of downtown. The earliness of the hour makes me lightheaded and, conscious of the feel of my hands on the wheel, I warn myself to drive carefully as I try to force myself awake. I am a little anxious, afraid some quirk of fate may prevent me from witnessing what I am on my way to see. At 6:30 A.M. Engineered Demolitions of Minneapolis is scheduled to blow up an ore bridge at the now-defunct Duquesne Works of U.S. Steel.

Headlights bear down behind me out of the darkness, approach with surprising speed to face me on the two-lane road that winds tight between the hill, like a canyon wall, to my right and the railroad tracks and river to my left. Across the river, a coke works is eerily luminescent, buildings highlighted by steam glowing in the plant's concatenation of lights. The news broadcast on the radio urges commuters to find an alternate route; the road past the mill will be closed before detonation of the blast. I ask myself why I didn't leave earlier. What if they close the road before I can get through? Seven miles from the city, I enter the town of Homestead, with the single line of stacks behind the buildings on Eighth Avenue, the old pump house at the Pinkerton landing site, virtually all that remains on a vast tract of land, of what was once the most famous steel mill in the world. So much of this steelmaking valley has been blasted, torched, and hauled away. I don't want to miss the demolition of the ore bridge. It is a way to bear witness and to pay my respects, a way to say good-bye.

My heart begins to beat faster as I approach Duquesne

and what remains of the nearly mile-long stretch of decaying plant sheds that precede the blast furnaces and the ore bridge. I am so nearly there, but can see in my mind's eye the police officer who may materialize before me to block my way. I draw reassurance from the fact that the traffic still moves smoothly toward me from up ahead. Finally, the blast furnaces, the stoves and stacks, the ore bridge emerge, silhouetted against the gray of the lightening sky. No one stops me, and, relieved, I pull into a shopping mall and park.

6:15 A.M. On the narrow sidewalk that borders the road, I press my back into the concrete retaining wall that holds the side of the hill. The traffic sweeps by, too close, at surely more than the thirty-five miles per hour that is the posted limit, and I retreat a little to the spot where the wall angles downward and levels, seat-high, to sit, scrunching backward into the hill.

An ore bridge is a giant moving crane, a sort of truss bridge on steel frame legs, like stilts. The one before me now stands reddish brown against the black of the huge, pear-shaped furnace behind it to which it once carried ore. A row of four cylindrical stoves stand at the furnace's side. Nearby, a gutted plant building, the former boiler shop, reveals its emptiness in the soft light showing in the tall, narrow windows lining its near and far sides. The plant grounds are tinged with the green of locust, sumac, and ailanthus.

6:23 A.M. The tiny silhouetted figure of a man walks along the bridge's top chord. He bends down near the center to check the wires to the explosives, then rises and moves on, then bends down again. Later, he retraces his steps, below on the bridge's lower span. In my blue jeans and cotton shirt I am beginning to feel the chill of the early morning. I look down at my arms beyond my rolled-up sleeves and see that I have goose bumps. A cricket begins its metallic chirp.

A man, in blue jeans too, and a Levi's jacket, approaches along the sidewalk, sturdy, bearlike, with wire-rimmed glasses and graying blond hair and beard. He smiles as he nears, then stops and looks across with me at the ore bridge.

"I guess nobody cares much about this any more," he says, noting that we are the only people here.

He worked at Duquesne for twenty-three years, he says, and his father worked there before him. He speaks angrily about U.S. Steel's closing of the mills and the brutal way in which it was done. He talks of being laid off from his most recent job, the lack of opportunity here. He says he is an electrician. He figures he'll put an ad in the paper.

We are quiet for a moment, just looking at the cluster of mill structures.

"I think they're beautiful," I say.

"They *are*," he replies emphatically.

An older man approaches and we exchange greetings. Standing face to face in front of me, the two men exclaim over the closing of the mills, how little management cared. As I look past them toward the mill site, I see the rhythmic bob of their heads out of the corner of my eye, as one speaks and the other nods in agreement.

Suddenly we realize that everything is quiet. The traffic has been stopped. As far as we can see, the road is a stretch of empty concrete. No one speaks. Two men in hard hats stand at a distance on the mill site. The hush is almost surreal, this utter silence, everything still.

7:07 A.M. A siren sounds. Then falls silent. The siren sounds again, longer this time, I think, then stops. After a moment another siren sounds, downriver, an echo. Then again all is silence.

When the blast comes it startles me. It is not the deep,

3

resonant sound I expected, but higher pitched, more of a crack. A gasping sob rises in my throat, surprises me, and I quash it. The center of the bridge has broken in two. Amid puffs of black smoke, the halves of the bridge's rent spans sink slightly to the center from each end. They hold there momentarily, then, pulling the legs along with them, fall toward each other to the ground. The smoke drifts, diffuses, into the sky. A siren sounds the all clear. The near half of the toppled bridge tips nose to the ground, its butt in the air. It was like watching someone get shot.

"They took the heart out of me when they shut the mills," the older man says. "We never cried about the dirt. It was bread on the table."

He tells me heatedly and fervently that Andrew Carnegie was his hero. Especially for his gift of the libraries. The Duquesne Works was part of the Carnegie Company's extensive holdings, which were valued at $480 million in 1901 with the merger that created U.S. Steel.

"What better gift could there be for the working man?" he exclaims. "A way for him to better himself."

The two of them turn again to the wrongs of the more recent past.

"It was all politics," they agree, as I try to take in the event we have just seen.

They wave good-bye and I look again at the fallen bridge. The rising sun lights the mist in the valley. The traffic sweeps by. I hear the cricket chirping again.

Prologue

Sunrise. A red-orange sun lifts out of a bank of clouds on the horizon, projecting a crystalline shaft of intense pink light upward through a luminous pink wash. Remnant dark clouds diffuse as they pass overhead in the white-blue sky.

It is in many ways an incomparably beautiful city. Houses spill in clusters over tree-covered hills, or nestle into hollows, their backs to the hillside. Countless creeks, or "runs," carve serpentine paths toward the valley floor and the three rivers that form the city's core. More than four hundred bridges span rivers, hollows, and runs.

I came home to Pittsburgh in the fall of 1990. Or rather, I came to live here for the first time. It was the place where generations of my family had lived, and where I had spent Christmas and summer vacations with my grandparents until they died. My father's company had moved him to Chicago before I was born. But Pittsburgh was our city. Our baseball team was the Pirates. The ketchup on our table was Heinz.

5

When I came back to Pittsburgh, I found an apartment at the edge of a bluff, overlooking the city's geographic and historical center. It is an almost unimaginably striking urban view. From floor-to-ceiling windows I look down on the confluence of the Allegheny and the Monongahela Rivers which join here to form the Ohio. I see the rivers just beyond the tips of my toes, though four hundred feet below. Their broad, gunmetal expanses converge before me in the form of a Y. The waters of the Allegheny have made their way from the north through forested Pennsylvania hills. The Monongahela, flowing north from its headwaters in West Virginia, follows a more industrial course. Its name, which is of Indian (probably Delaware) origin, is said to mean "falling-in banks."

Looking out over the rivers it is impossible not to feel their might, or to avoid the thought that their convergence here is a part of some destiny. Within the triangle of land between the converging rivers I see the four-bastioned outline in stone that commemorates Fort Duquesne, the tiny earth and timber fort that was built here by the French in 1754. Nearby, as the triangle widens, is a recreated bastion of the brawnier Fort Pitt, whose construction was begun five years later by the English after their victory over the French. Behind these traces of its eighteenth-century past, and still within the triangle formed by the rivers, stand the hallmarks of the city's twentieth-century present, downtown skyscrapers of steel, aluminum, and glass, materials that have been elemental to the identity of Pittsburgh, its economic bedrock.

The scene from my window is in part still a basic industrial landscape. Towboats push barges of coal along the rivers, in rows, three or four abreast like great flat rafts. A single standard barge measures 175 feet long by 26 feet wide and carries over 900 tons, 1.8 million pounds, of coal. (I have seen a single towboat pushing up to twenty barges at a time—over 36 million pounds.) Trains move east and west on the tracks along the near side of the "Mon," carrying coal, piggybacking semi-trailers, or hauling other freight. A variety of bridges spans the rivers—tied-arch, lenticular truss, eyebar chain suspension, and more. I can see nineteen in all from my window.

The hill I live on is scaled by two funiculars, or inclines. They are run by electricity now, rather than steam. One, the Duquesne Incline, originally called the Duquesne Inclined Plane, was constructed in 1877. It still has its original cable drum and its original wooden-toothed drive gear. Replacement teeth of aged rock maple are kept on hand for drive gear repairs. The bright red cars, with their amber clerestory windows and hand-carved interior panels, date to 1889. I can see the cars from my window, jutting out on the horizontal from the thirty-degree angle of their tracks.

I look out on a place far different from the place that Pittsburgh was. Plant buildings once dominated the narrow flats along the rivers. Night skies were lit by fire. The city throbbed with the pounding energy of heavy industrial work. As early as 1803 iron was its most important industry. By 1850 a larger proportion of its population worked in heavy manufacturing than in any other American city. In 1883, Willard Glazier wrote of Pittsburgh's "four hundred and seventy-eight manufactories of iron, steel, cotton, brass, oil, glass, copper and wood," which were contained in "a distance of thirty-five and one-half miles of streets." By 1894 Pittsburgh and its environs produced 30 percent of the nation's steel. In this century airline pilots used the glow of Pittsburgh's furnaces as a marker in dark night skies.

Much of the nation's material greatness came out of Pittsburgh. Steel rails, structural shapes, sheet and plate, forgings for the machinery of an industrial age. George Westinghouse came to Pittsburgh to manufacture his airbrake, which would make railroad travel and transport practical and safe (the increased braking power meant that a train could be heavier and faster). A great inventive mind, who would earn more than 350 patents over a lifetime, he subsequently pioneered the use of alternating current (AC) over direct (DC), which was favored by Thomas Edison. His Westinghouse Electric Company manufactured the huge generators, the transformers, the meters, and other elements of an AC system that would revolutionize the generation and transmission of electrical power.

Pittsburgh was a city that put ideas to work. In 1888, Charles Martin Hall and Arthur Vining Davis poured the first commercial aluminum ingot at the Pittsburgh Reduction Company on Smallman Street. The company was the forerunner of Alcoa. Thomas Mellon and his sons provided financing for Henry Clay Frick's tremendous coking operations and such eventual local corporate giants as Alcoa, Koppers, Carborundum, and Gulf Oil. I have read that as recently as the 1970s every family in the country was touched by Pittsburgh in some way, every day.

Still, Pittsburgh was synonymous with steel. Between 1899 and 1947, 70 to 75 percent of Pittsburgh's manufacturing was in steel and other metals; during World War II area mills produced ninety-five million tons of steel. For much of its history, mills and foundries hugged the riverbanks—long plant sheds with sloping roofs punctuated by rows of jutting stacks, with workers' housing, commercial buildings, and churches hard by. Nearby river towns—Homestead, Rankin, Braddock, Duquesne, McKeesport, Clairton, Monessen, Aliquippa— existed almost solely to make steel. In the valley of the

Monongahela, steel mills extended upriver from Pittsburgh for forty-six miles.

Now, most of the area's former steelmaking capacity is gone. By the end of the 1980s miles of furnaces and plant buildings stood silent, awaiting demolition. Vast stretches of land stand vacant even now, as efforts are made to attract new, cleaner, and inevitably smaller industries. Big Steel shed up to 90 percent of its work force here during its massive retrenchment of the 1970s and 1980s. U.S. Steel alone eliminated more than thirty thousand jobs. It is estimated that for each primary job lost, two to three additional jobs are lost in related industries and local neighborhood stores. During the period, other former industrial giants closed down, most notably the vast Westinghouse Electric Corporation works in East Pittsburgh. All told, more than forty major industrial plants closed here during the 1980s. One hundred and thirty thousand jobs were lost; 176,000 people left. Of the displaced workers who remained, 25 percent found equivalent jobs, 50 percent found lesser jobs, and 25 percent were unemployed at the end of the decade. By the end of the decade the area had lost 14 percent of its young.

The city of Pittsburgh, in which steel's presence had already diminished over time and which was in any event more diversified, has withstood the hit—at least for now. The future of the nearby steelmaking towns is more uncertain. As I write, Big Steel is making a comeback, but with new technologies that require significantly fewer workers. And new plants, for the most part, are going elsewhere. Today, we face a compelling need to bring jobs to the area if we are to keep our children here.

I had not planned to move to Pittsburgh. The city was part

of my past, and it was only by accident that I rediscovered it. In the fall of 1990, the Pirates were playing the Cincinnati Reds in the National League playoffs and my brother, who lives in Baltimore, suggested that we meet in Pittsburgh to attend the middle three games of the best-of-seven series. I had not been in Pittsburgh for years. At the time, I was recovering from the death of my husband a little over a year and a half before, and I was still at something of a loss, wondering if there was a place in the world for me. I knew I didn't want to start again in New York, where I had lived for twenty years, without him. On a sunny afternoon before one of the games I found myself on Mt. Washington, the hill that rises abruptly across the river from downtown and the hill on which I now live. I looked out over the city in the hazy sunlight. The air was nearly still, and I felt almost suspended above the rivers and buildings below. As I sat there, my mind just drifting, I was suddenly suffused with a sense that things had come right, that I understood who I was and where I belonged. I was suddenly acutely aware that this was my city. I felt the city somehow almost literally inside of me. I did not try to analyze what was happening. I simply knew that I had come home. I remember looking past the coal barges across from the Point (as the tip of the triangle between the rivers is called) and down the Ohio. The stacks and storage tanks of Neville Island were just visible in the distance. I had passed the site often as a child, sitting in the backseat as my grandfather drove my brother and me into Pittsburgh. The sight of its industrial installations, which I had seen so many times long ago, sealed my sense of peace.

In 1985 Rand McNally called Pittsburgh "the most livable city in the United States." Non-Pittsburghers guffawed. The headline in the *Washington Post* read "Pittsburgh? No. 1? Gimme a Break!" The Pittsburgh of the public mind was smoky, grimy, a "hell with the lid off." Though not entirely representative, photographs of streetlights shining in the smoky darkness of noon were legend. But the image was thirty years out of date. Smoke controls passed in the early 1940s and put into effect after the war had largely eliminated the smoke. Mills and factories worked under increasingly stringent environmental controls. Local government and private corporations had collaborated in two redevelopment efforts—called Renaissance I and Renaissance II—to rebuild the city's center.

I am proud of the city's resilience, of those sparkling, top-lit towers downtown. But I remain grieved by what was suffered here as Big Steel all but closed down. The area still boasts a number of smaller, specialized steel companies, as well as producers of stainless and other alloy steels, but only one of the historic integrated mills—the combined Edgar Thomson and Irvin Works of U.S. Steel—survives. Projected newer mills and shops will require only a fraction of the workers once employed in steel.

We seem, as a nation, to lose our industrial places with such equanimity. For many of us, if we think of them at all, they are places apart, intrusions on the landscape we'd just as soon see in someone else's neighborhood or someone else's town. We have little thought for the workers whose lives are shattered by a plant closing. They are people whom most of us don't even know. The loss, if it is mourned at all, is mourned for its effect on the economy. But I believe it is important that we understand the industrial landscape. It is important for us to realize that when we lose our industrial places we lose more than we may be aware of, that the loss is more than economic, and experienced by more than those most immediately involved. The industrial experience is elemental to the human experience. When we lose our industrial places we lose a vital part of who we are.

We are not accustomed to thinking in such terms nowadays. When we think of industry we think of air pollution and toxic waste and the holes in the ozone layer. And of course we must. I do not mean to suggest that unspeakable things have not been done to the landscape in the name of industry, or that industry should be allowed to operate free of environmental controls. On the contrary. Our only justification comes with a deep respect for landscape and a sense of limits. I only mean to say that there is value in industrial landscapes and it is important for us to know what it is.

Sitting on that hillside overlooking the city, I thought back to my childhood and the disparaging remarks I often heard, still hear, from those who don't know them, about Pittsburgh and other industrial landscapes. Recognizing this landscape as my home, I felt a profound sadness in the face of our willingness to let industrial places go, and to let them go without regard for what they are, or were. And so I set out to investigate the industrial landscape and to tell the human story represented here. I will focus in this book on Pittsburgh, but elements of the story have played out in myriad other industrial cities—Buffalo, Youngstown, Cleveland, Baltimore, parts of Chicago, among others, and residents of those cities will recognize or find parallels to their own cities here. This book is intended not simply as a story of Pittsburgh, but as a search for the heart of the industrial landscape using Pittsburgh as a lens. We tend nowadays to seek answers in wilderness. What we neglect or remain unaware of is what has been honorable and good in industrial life. We neglect the lessons we can learn there about leading a good life—about life in community, about the meaning of physical work, about what it is that ties us to landscape, about the act of being and living in a place. We may continue to lose our industrial landscapes. What we should not lose is their story.

The view from my window is a pageant of water

and light. The river waters are still as glass today,

Out of This Land

reflecting the fretted curve

of Three Rivers Stadium

across from the Point, the evergreen and deciduous

trees along the riverbanks, the arch of the Fort Pitt

Bridge turned golden bronze in its reverse image on

the surface of the water. The gray of the sky at the

hilltops lightens overhead to a pale, delicate gray

blue, marked by darker, apparently motionless puffs

of cloud.

Pittsburgh is a city profoundly aware of its landscape. Pedestrians cross the bridges over the rivers
on foot. Long flights of steps scale hills too steep
for simple paths. Streets, many of them narrow,
plunge, soar, and careen off at angles in deference
to the terrain. When I turn off the rim of my hill to
drive down the back slope, I look into the rearview
mirror and see only sky.

Access to downtown from the south is by tunnel under the long ridge called Mt. Washington. Travelers enter as if through the portal of a medieval city, struck by the rivers and bridges, sparkling towers, and light whose existence they could scarcely have suspected from the other side of the hill. It is as if the hills themselves were the center city's walls. Sitting on a grassy portion at the top of the hillside, at night, looking out over the city, I have felt physically the power and richness of the land, as my body bore down into the solidity of that earth. I have thought of the coal that the land beneath me has given, its gift.

The broad outlines of the city's story are evident in something as simple as a road map. I have formed the habit of spreading my map of Pennsylvania on the living room floor next to the window. The map reminds me of where I am and why a city was founded here and why it thrived. On hands and knees, I trace the intricate, meandering paths of the Allegheny and the Monongahela, curving, circling back on themselves as they make their way toward the city. Road patterns to the east become a succession of arcs between the Appalachian mountain ridges that separate Pittsburgh from the cities of the Atlantic seaboard. Towns with names like Coal Center and Cokeburg denote the area's vast seams of bituminous coal and its transformation into coke. Early blast furnace sites still dot the landscape—Lemont Furnace, Oliphant Furnace, Wharton Furnace, once small-scale smelters of local iron ore. Their charcoal-burning furnaces of brick and stone were rural forerunners of the looming industrial giants to come. Two hours by car to the north, the town of Oil City recalls "Colonel" Edwin L. Drake, who sank the world's first oil well nearby at Titusville in 1859. Pittsburgh grew up in an era when geology and geography mattered more to the prosperity of cities, before faxes and e-mail and FedEx allowed cities to grow largely outside the context of work. Pittsburgh's story, like that of most older industrial cities, grew out of, and because of, the land. More specifically, Pittsburgh's destiny grew out of its bedrock, the mountain barrier, and the flow of its rivers. As I look at my road map, I realize that my understanding of the city is inseparable from what I have learned of its origins and the path it followed in becoming an industrial place.

The city's valleys and hills are the eroded surface of the system of nearly horizontal sedimentary layers that we call the Appalachian Plateau. Layers of bedrock reveal themselves along the river cliffs and along roadways and railroads cut into the hillsides—shale, sandstone, marine and freshwater limestones, clay, and coal. Soldiers from Fort Pitt hauled chunks of coal from the bluff along the Monongahela by canoe as early as 1759 or 1760. James Kenny, assistant to the agent of the trading post at Fort Pitt, wrote in his journal in May 1761, "I & my brother & two other Men went to see yᵉ Coal Pit on land in ye Mountain Side over yᵉ Monongahela; yᵉ Mountain is so high & steep that its with Care & difficulty people gets up to it, but its easy got, as . . . yᵉ Coal is in a Bank fronting like a upright Wall in yᵉ Hill side they put it into bags & tumbles them down yᵉ hill." Outcrops from "Coal Hill," now Mt. Washington, were part of the Pittsburgh Coal, the most significant of the region's many layers, extending through eastern Ohio, western Pennsylvania, West Virginia, and Maryland, and mined over an area of six thousand square miles. Even after two hundred years of mining, it has been called the earth's single most valuable coal deposit.

The coal that was to provide the city with steam for power and coke for iron smelting formed slowly, at the leisured pace of geologic time, in tropical swamps that bordered a vast inland sea. The Pennsylvanian coal forest was a land of giant dragonflies, cockroaches, and centipedes, of huge amphibians, and reptiles like the fin-backed *Edaphosaurus*. The straight trunks of *Lepidodendron* reached a hundred feet to the sky amid a variety of plants, including seed ferns, cordaites, tree ferns, and calamites. As plants died and sank into the swamp, more plants grew over them and died in turn. Layer upon layer the plant debris accumulated, along with intervening layers of sediment, the upper layers generating the heat and pressure to compact the plant layers below, over millions of years, first into peat, then into lignite, and then, in the case of Pittsburgh, into bituminous coal. A ten-foot layer like the Pittsburgh Coal would have required a plant buildup of at least two hundred feet. At Pittsburgh's Carnegie Museum of Natural History a slice of bituminous coal, enlarged eight hundred times, reveals its source in the yellows of embedded plant spores, resin, and cuticle; in the red of coalized wood and bark; and in the black of plant material that has been carbonized. It has been calculated that before mining began, Allegheny County, of which Pittsburgh is the county seat, had 3,194,820,000 tons of bituminous coal.

During the Pennsylvanian Period, between 320 and 286 million years ago, the area that is Pittsburgh was near the equator, near the eastern edge of the North American plate. At approximately mid-period, the North American and African plates collided, thrusting upward the Appalachians and the Mauritanian Mountains of West Africa in a process of mountain building called the Alleghenian orogeny. Vast rivers and streams carried sediments eroded from the mountains—sands, silts, and clays—toward the inland sea that extended over the future site of Pittsburgh. As the sea advanced and retreated over the coal swamps, sedimentary deposits were laid down to become limestones, sandstones, and shales. Millions of microorganisms also living in the sea eventually combined with the accumulating sediments to form oil and gas.

The coal measures of western Pennsylvania are for the most part Pennsylvanian in origin, that is, so well developed and described that the term *Pennsylvanian* is applied everywhere to them and to rocks of similar age. Our terms for eras of geologic time are merely that, of course—our terms. Without thinking I sometimes feel a wave of disappointment as I remind myself that terms like Pennsylvanian, Ordovician, Jurassic, which are so rich to the tongue and to the ear, are simply modern inventions, terms that *we* have devised. I find myself wanting to know what the real names of those periods are, what they were called at the time, forgetting that names are only human.

With the laying down of the coal and the upward thrust of the Appalachians, two elements of the city's geological triad had come into being. It would be several hundred million years before the final element, the drainage of the rivers, would be established.

Before the Pleistocene, or Ice Age, between 1.8 million and ten thousand years ago, Pittsburgh's rivers followed far different paths. The ancestral Ohio and the southernmost of three rivers that have since combined to form the Allegheny were tributaries of the Monongahela, which flowed northward over its entire course to empty into the ancestral Lake Erie Basin. The "upper Allegheny" and the "middle Allegheny" flowed northward into the basin as well. The glaciers of the Pleistocene, sheets of ice as thick as two miles, advanced from the north, stopping short of Pittsburgh but acting as dams in the rivers. As ice blocked the rivers, lakes formed along the glaciers' edge, which in turn pushed backward into the riverbeds as their waters grew too high to be contained. Erosion, enhanced by meltwater and glacial debris, maintained the southerly flow and the drainage we take for granted today. I can see traces of the preglacial pattern on my road map, as the Ohio heads northwest out of Pittsburgh before turning back south to make its journey west. With the westward thrust of the rivers, the geological triad was complete, and the scene was set for manufacture west of the mountains and for trade with floods of settlers passing through.

In their journals eighteenth-century travelers wrote of standing at the summit of the Allegheny Front, the eastern escarpment of the Alleghenies (the Appalachian mountain ridges which are closest to Pittsburgh), and looking west over a sea of trees. The forests were dense with oak and sugar maple, chestnut, walnut, and hickory. In northern portions of the area, two-hundred-foot stands of hemlock merged into similar stands of white pine. Grapevines laced through the treetops, roofing the forest and wreathing it in darkness. Legend has it that a squirrel could make his way from Philadelphia to Pittsburgh without ever touching the ground.

It was a landscape larger and richer than life, or life as we know it. John Heckewelder, a Moravian missionary, wrote in 1789 of "a wild cherry tree on the bank of the Allegheny . . . 18 feet in circumference," of plums and large wild apples, of honey locusts along the river bottoms and beside the streams. Nicholas Cresswell agreed: "Walnut and Cherry Trees grow to an amazing size. I have seen several three foot [in] diameter and 40 foot before they come to a limb." Colonel John May reported that "within 10 rods of the house [at the foot of Coal Hill], we can catch any quantity of fish we want, and almost any kind—in particular Cat fish, Perch, Buffelow, Pike, Bass of two sorts, sturgeon's of two sorts etc." He noted one catfish that weighed 120 pounds, adding that "he drownd the man that took him." An unidentified French traveler wrote of the beautiful black squirrels swimming in the water near Fort Duquesne, of "hummingbirds hardly as big as olives," of fireflies and swarms of bees. The wife of a settler reported the presence of "some panthers and many wolves." Game was plentiful: deer, elk, wood buffalo, bear, and appearing again and again in the accounts of early travelers, wild turkeys, weighing as much as thirty or forty pounds. Christian Schultz Jr. described them in 1807 as "so overburthened with fat that they fly with difficulty. It frequently happens," he wrote, "that after shooting one on a tree, you will find him bursted by falling on the ground."

I saw a glimpse of this past, if only a glimpse, two hours from the city in Cook Forest Park, a Registered National Natural Landmark, which contains some of the oldest stands of virgin white pine and hemlock in the northeast. Along the trails, tall, straight trunks of white pine, once used for ship masts, stand thick with towering trunks of hemlock, their leafless lower branches truncated like the arms of a scarecrow. A burst of branches high above forms a filigree of green illumined by the sun, in contrast to the comparative dim of the forest floor. As far as I could tell, the treetops had no vines.

Cook Forest is an old-age or climax forest. Older trees are dying. Many simply fall over, pulling a fringe of roots from the soil. When I put my hand on a massive trunk lying along the ground, its moss-covered curve felt like an animal's flank.

When prospective white settlers first arrived, the area near the Point was only sparsely settled by native peoples. Much of what is now western Pennsylvania had been reserved since 1656 as a hunting ground by the Iroquois, who had driven out its previous inhabitants. Its repopulation had begun in the early 1700s as native groups sought new lands, largely in response to the pressure of whites moving west. A trader's census shows the Delaware chief Senangel and sixteen families at Shannopin's Town, two miles upriver on the Allegheny. (The site is now occupied by the Pittsburgh neighborhood of Lawrenceville.) Queen Allaquippa reigned "with great authority" over a small band of Seneca at the modern site of McKees Rocks, a few miles down the Ohio, before moving on to the Monongahela and the mouth of the "Yough" (short for Youghiogheny River, and so called even in the eighteenth century, pronounced *Yock*). Shingas, another Delaware leader, succeeded Queen Allaquippa at McKees Rocks. Shawnee, Delaware, and Mingo lived eighteen miles down the Ohio at Logstown (near modern-day Ambridge, named for the American Bridge Company), which also served as a headquarters for English traders and as a site of negotiation between Indians and whites. Most of its forty log cabins had been built for the Indians by the French.

Historians Solon and Elizabeth Buck have written of the "Arcadian quality in Indian life as it existed in western Pennsylvania in the second quarter of the eighteenth century. It was a life of leisure, of hospitality, of a simple social honesty." A stranger or friend was greeted with a haunch of venison or at least a communal pipe. White traders plied their wares in the area, exchanging a range of goods, most significantly guns, ammunition, and rum, for the Indians' furs and skins. George Croghan, a former Dubliner who was married to a native woman and was said to control a fourth of the Ohio country trade, had a trading post across the Allegheny from Shannopin's Town, and another down the Ohio at Logstown. John Frazier's trading post stood a hundred yards east of the steep bank of the Monongahela at Turtle Creek, on land given to him by Queen Allaquippa.

When George Washington arrived in November 1753, there were no native settlements on the land between the Forks, that is, the Point. (At the time, the converging Allegheny and Monongahela were referred to as the Forks of the Ohio.) Perhaps because it could be swampy and subject to flood, it was not as highly prized by native peoples as other sites. Washington was on a mission to Fort Le Boeuf, now Waterford in Erie County, to deliver the British response to the recent military advance by the French into the Ohio country. The French, wishing to secure the most direct route between their dominions in Canada and the city of New Orleans, had moved early in 1753 toward the Ohio, building forts at Presque Isle, now Erie, and Lake Le Boeuf. The British, who were unwilling to have their colonies in the New World hemmed in by the Appalachians, instructed the governors of Pennsylvania, Maryland, and Virginia to demand that the French withdraw, or to "repel Force by Force" if they declined. They also authorized Governor Dinwiddie of Virginia to build forts along the Ohio. (The southern and western borders of Pennsylvania were not permanently fixed until 1779; until then, the lands north to the Ohio were claimed as well by Virginia.) Dinwiddie chose the "gentleman" George Washington to deliver the message to the French and to evaluate the proposal by the Ohio Company, a group of Virginia land speculators, to build a fort near the Forks. Washington's guide, Christopher Gist, had made several previous trips for the company, and in June of 1752, with three commissioners appointed by the Virginia governor, had distributed a present to the Indians at Logstown. In return, the Indians had granted permission to build two forts.

Of that day in November 1753, at the future site of Pitts-burgh, Washington wrote in his journal, "I spent some Time in viewing the Rivers, and the Land in the Fork; which I think extremely well situated for a Fort, as it has the absolute Com-mand of both Rivers. The Land at the Point is 20 or 25 Feet above the common Surface of the Water; and a considerable Bottom of flat, well-timbered Land all around it, very conve-nient for Building: The Rivers are each a Quarter of a Mile, or more, across, and run here very near at right Angles: *Aligany* bearing N.E. and *Monongahela* S.E. The former of these two is a very rapid and swift running Water; the other deep and still, without any perceptible Fall."

After considering and rejecting the Ohio Company's pre-vious choice of site, at the place where "lives *Shingiss*, King of the *Delawares*," Washington forged on to Fort Le Boeuf and delivered Governor Dinwiddie's letter requiring the "peaceable Departure" of the French. In reply the fort's commander was gracious but firm: "As to the Summons you send me to retire, I do not think myself obliged to obey."

The following year found a small force of Virginians en-gaged in construction at the Forks of Fort Prince George (the first British fort on the triangle of land beneath my window). The Virginians were unaware, however, of the approach down the Allegheny of the French captain Pierre de Contrecoeur and his five hundred troops. Contrecoeur arrived on April 16 with three hundred canoes and sixty bateaux and disembarked at Shannopin's Town. Moving toward the Point the following day, the troops trained their cannon on the fort and demanded the surrender of its defenders. Given the superiority of the French in number and arms, the Virginians obediently retired.

The French demolished Fort Prince George and erected in its place the earth and timber, four-bastioned structure they called Fort Duquesne.

Even as the French were dismantling Fort Prince George, two companies of Virginia militia, unaware of its fall to the French, were making their way from Alexandria to the Forks of the Ohio as reinforcements. The troops' commander, George Washington, this time in military guise, learned at Fort Cumberland (Maryland) that Fort Prince George had fallen. He did not turn back, however, but proceeded on, engaging a small detachment of the enemy fifty miles south of the Forks near Chestnut Ridge. During the rout, which lasted only fifteen minutes, twelve French soldiers, including their commander, Coulon de Jumonville, were killed, and the rest were taken prisoner. Washington wrote in his journal, "If the whole Detachment of the French behave with no more Resolution than this chosen Party did, I flatter myself we shall have no great Trouble in driving them to . . . Montreal." It was the first battle of what we have come to call the French and Indian War.

We know of course that Washington's confidence was misplaced. Only weeks later, deserted by his Indian allies, he was in full retreat at Fort Necessity. A quarter of his force was ill from hunger and exhaustion. The subsequent attack by six hundred soldiers and one hundred Indians led by Coulon de Villiers, Jumonville's brother, began at noon and ended eight hours later and left Washington with such heavy losses that he had little choice but to accept Villiers's terms of capitulation.

It was not the last defeat to be suffered by the British in their effort to reclaim the Point. On July 9, 1755, a large British force under the command of Major-General Edward Braddock was massacred near Turtle Creek by French troops and their Indian allies. Nearly one thousand of approximately fourteen hundred British troops were killed or wounded. Almost two decades later the Reverend David McClure would write in his diary, "Monday rode to Braddock's field. . . . It was a melancholy spectacle to see the bones of men strewed over the ground, left to this day, without the solemn rite of sepulture." (Since the 1870s, the battlefield has been the site of the Edgar Thomson steel plant.)

In September 1758, an even larger British force was moving toward the Forks under the command of Brigadier General John Forbes. Their progress was slow, as Forbes had decided not to travel to the Forks by Braddock's route northwest from Virginia, but to cut a new road straight over the Pennsylvania mountains, building or enlarging forts along the way. It was from the army's advance camp at Loyalhanna that Major James Grant moved out with 750 troops, including 300 Highlanders, to reconnoitre Fort Duquesne and possibly recover some prisoners. Once within range of the fort, Grant gave in to a (somewhat Custerlike) overassessment of his strength and guile and moved to lure its occupants into ambush from the hill that would subsequently bear his name. Three hundred men were killed, thirty-seven, including Grant, taken prisoner. The heads of several decapitated Highlanders were soon impaled on stakes along the Indian racetrack outside the fort, their kilts draped underneath.

In spite of the humiliation of Grant, there was no denying the superior strength of Forbes's army, of which the French were well aware. Their Indian allies were equally aware and preferred to retire to their autumn hunting grounds in face of the British threat. By late November, some were even negotiating a peace with the Moravian missionary Christian Frederick Post at their camp across the Allegheny from Fort Duquesne. When the British forces arrived at the Point, they found the fort deserted, its timbers smoldering. The French had burned it to the ground.

General Forbes surveyed the scene the following day from a litter that had been suspended between two horses (Forbes had to travel by litter through the entire campaign). He was exhausted and weak with "the bloody flux," and only months short of dying. Summoning his strength, he dictated the opening of a letter to William Pitt, then a secretary of state and in charge of the North American campaign: "Sir, I do myself the honour of acquainting you that it has pleased God to crown His Majesty's Arms with Success over all his Enemies upon the Ohio." Concluding the letter some weeks later, he added, "I have used the freedom of giving your name to Fort Du Quesne, as I hope it was in some measure the being actuated by your spirits that now makes us Masters of the place." The letter was dated "Pittsbourgh, 27 Novem. 1758."

Pitt responded with orders to erect a fort at the Point "strong enough to assure the undisputed possession of the Ohio," and in August 1759 General John Stanwix arrived to oversee its construction. In my mind's eye I see the swarm of activity as the Point came alive with brick kilns, saw pits, and forges, and the works for the "largest and costliest" of British forts in North America displaced the ruins of Fort Duquesne. The completed Fort Pitt covered seventeen and a half acres with its outworks included. One and a quarter million locally fired, whitish bricks went into its construction. Behind the fort was a village of approximately 150 houses and at least a third as many "huts." The Union Jack proclaimed its authority from a pole rising above the flag bastion. One modern drawing of the fort lists thirteen buildings, including a barracks that measured 180 feet in length.

The newly completed fort marked the toehold of a culture

largely antithetical to that of the area's native peoples. Similarly, their ways were incompatible with and perhaps incomprehensible to the white settlers who would follow. The life of the native hunter required vast tracts of uncultivated land, while for the whites ownership of land was the standard by which people were defined. Hugh Henry Brackenridge, a Princeton-educated lawyer and chronicler of early Pittsburgh, expressed the settlers' point of view: "It was against [the] laws of God and nature that so much land should lie idle while so many christians wanted it to work on and to raise their bread." Though it was the policy of the British government, the Pennsylvania Assembly, and the commandants at Fort Pitt to prevent settlement west and south of the Forks and to reserve those lands as native hunting grounds, the steady influx of settlers rendered the policy unenforceable. With the Treaty of Fort Stanwix of 1768, by which the Iroquois ceded their claim to lands in the southwestern portion of the state, the policy was abandoned. By 1775, in spite of continued danger of attack by Indians still resisting their advance, at least fifty thousand people had settled south of the Forks.

Pittsburgh, after the Revolution, was a rowdy, independent-minded place, short on the refinements of the eastern seaboard. Its houses, most of them built of logs, were often ramshackle, its streets often seas of mud. "Sanitary provisions were primitive," writes historian Leland Baldwin, "the dogs made night hideous with their howls, and drunken Indians and whites snored beside hogs in the mud puddles." During his visit to Pittsburgh in 1788, John May wrote in his journal, "I have had but little sleep since I have been here chiefly owing to the barking of dogs. I believe here are two dogs to one man—and at my quarters there are no less than seventeen of these wide throated son's of B—."

Still, the seeds of civility were being planted. The *Pittsburgh Gazette,* the first newspaper west of the Alleghenies, was established in 1786. In 1787, the Pittsburgh Academy, which would eventually become the University of Pittsburgh, was incorporated to teach "the Learned Languages, English, and the Mathematicks." A German evangelical church was organized in 1782; the Presbyterian congregation of Pittsburgh was incorporated in 1787. Prominent families like the Nevilles and the O'Haras provided a degree of elegance and polish. A visitor from Philadelphia, Mrs. Mary Dewees, described "Mr. and Mrs. O'Harra" as "very polite and agreeable." On a call to "Col. Butler and his lady," she noted the "very handsome parlour, elegantly papered and well furnished, . . . more like Philadelphia than any I have seen since I left that place." Before long the town would boast several music teachers and a store that sold violins.

But the city's identity would be forged above all by its situation and the wealth of the land. Fertile soil soon created agricultural surpluses that could be converted to capital or exchanged in trade, shipped down the Ohio and the Mississippi by keelboat, flatboat, or barge. By 1800 the "Gateway to the West" was shipping "flour, whiskey, bar iron and castings, glass, salted pork and beef, copper and tin wares, cordage, apples, cider, and peach and apple brandy" downriver to New Orleans. The mountains to the east were as good as a tariff, so hazardous and expensive was it to transport goods over them. Settlers often sold everything before leaving the eastern seaboard, then, once over the mountains, bought flatboats and otherwise outfitted themselves at Pittsburgh, the meeting-place of overland and river routes to the west. Flatboats could be had in Pittsburgh boatyards at a dollar a foot, to be broken up for lumber at their final destination. Local manufactories grew up in face of the cost of goods from the east. On the subject of glass, Joshua Gilpin, a Philadelphia investor, wrote in his journal, "the cost of this article when procured at Philadelphia would be more than doubled by carriage to Pittsburgh since a black glass bottle which costs 5 cents would require 6 more to convey it.—add to this that there is no article whose price is so exceedingly inhanced by accident.—it could rarely happen that a crate of bottles could pass over the mountains without a large portion of it being broken." By 1797, James O'Hara and Isaac Craig had established Pittsburgh's first glass factory on Coal Hill, using coal from a seam near the summit of the hill to manufacture "black & green glass principally bottles & window glass."

The land offered timber for logs and lumber, and for charcoal to be used in iron smelting. It offered clay for bricks, limestone and sand for glass, iron ore, and coal—for manufacturing and eventually for steam-powered transport. William Turnbull began construction of western Pennsylvania's first iron furnace in 1789 on Jacob's Creek in Fayette County, to Pittsburgh's south. In 1802 Zadok Cramer, another chronicler of early Pittsburgh, noted the presence of one brewery, two glassworks, a paper mill, several oil mills, fulling mills, powderworks, ironworks, saltworks, sawmills, gristmills, and boatyards. By 1817, Cramer's *Pittsburgh Magazine Almanack* listed the products of the city's iron manufacture: "nails, shovels, tongs, spades, scythes, sickles, hoes, axes, frying pans, cutting knives, vices, scale beams, augers, chisels, nail springs, locks, files, coffee mills, plane bits, door handles," and numerous other articles. By 1809 the city had its first steam-powered flour mill. The steam engine's finer parts were manufactured in Philadelphia, then shipped to Pittsburgh where they were assembled under the supervision of George Evans, the son of Oliver Evans, with parts that could be manufactured locally. By 1816, at least eight steam engines were in use in Pittsburgh's mills or factories, the largest being the seventy-horsepower engine at Cowan's rolling and slitting mill. Cramer's *Almanack* of 1817 observed that local manufacturing "has almost rendered us as independent of the eastern states, as those states have been rendered by the war independent of the Old World."

The city grew dramatically. The Scottish geographer and merchant John Melish noted that by 1810 Pittsburgh "contained 11 stone buildings, 283 of brick, and 473 of frame and log; making in all 767; and the number of inhabitants was 4768." Public buildings included "a court-house, jail, market-house, bank, academy, and 5 places of public worship." Even then, the city drew character from its work. "In the course of my walks through the streets," Melish recalled, "I heard every where the sound of the hammer and anvil; all was alive; every thing indicated the greatest industry, and attention to business." Yet the city could be beautiful. "I ascended a handsome eminence, called Grant's Hill," Melish wrote, "from whence I had a fine view of the town and country." A sketch of the Point drawn in 1817 by Mrs. James Gibson of Philadelphia while on her wedding trip shows a cluster of clean, trim houses and steepled churches, framed by rolling, tree-lined hills, with a flatboat on the river in the foreground and a single smoking stack on the city side of the Mon.

Not all observers were as sanguine. Of his visit to the city in 1816, David Thomas wrote that *"Pittsburgh* was hidden from our view, until we descended through the hills within half a mile of the *Allegany* river. Dark dense smoke was rising from many parts, and a hovering cloud of this vapour, obscuring the prospect, rendered it singularly gloomy." Ten days later Thomas left Pittsburgh, "with all the joy of a bird which escapes from its cage." The Englishman John Bernard wrote that "on approaching Pittsburgh we were struck with a peculiarity nowhere else to be observed in the States; a cloud of smoke hung over it in an exceedingly clear sky, recalling to me many choking recollections of London." Another Englishman, John Pearson, called the city "a poor, gloomy, sickly receptacle, hardly fit for convicts of the worst description." And yet, he wrote, "this was the place where the hammers stunned your ears, and the manufactories struck you dumb with astonishment." Nonetheless, rather than buy a farm and settle down as he had intended, he promptly turned around and returned to England.

Others perceived the positive beyond the smoke. Russell Errett, a newspaperman and politician, recalled that after first seeing Pittsburgh, the initial gloom and melancholy the city inspired "passed away never to return." Decades later, Anthony Trollope called the city "without exception, the blackest place which I ever saw," then proceeded to vindicate it: "Nothing can be more picturesque than the site," he wrote. "Even the filth and wondrous blackness of the place are picturesque when looked down upon from above. . . . I was never more in love with smoke and dirt than when I stood here and watched the darkness of night close in upon the floating soot which hovered over the house-tops of the city." Cramer's *Navigator* of 1817 observed that "the character of the people is that of enterprising and persevering industry." From the city's earliest days, smoke not only issued from household chimneys, but also signified that people were at work.

And that, above all, has been what Pittsburgh is about— work. A vein of Calvinism ran deep from its beginnings, in the Presbyterianism of the dominant Scots and Scotch-Irish founding population. Years later James Parton would write that "the masters of Pittsburgh are mostly of Scotch-Irish race, . . . keen and steady in the prosecution of their affairs, indifferent to pleasure, singularly devoid of the usual vanities and ostentations, proud to possess a solid and spacious factory, and to live in an insignificant house. There are no men of leisure in the town." (History would contradict Parton in one respect. Pittsburgh's Gilded Age industrial millionaires would build houses that were anything but "insignificant.")

The verve of this trans-Appalachian frontier was most visibly manifest in the keelboatmen, tough, roisterous, independent, who moved farm produce and other freight along the rivers. Poling their shallow craft, or hauling them from shore, warping (pulling from the boat on ropes tied to trees), or bushwhacking (reaching from the bow for a branch along the riverbank, then walking aft to propel the boat upstream), they were, until overtaken by steam, the rivers' mighty men. Tall tales and hyperbole swelled around such real-life adventurers as Cherry Tree Joe McCreery and Mike Fink, making them the stuff of legend.

Cherry Tree Joe, who hailed from the town of Cherry Tree, was the more genial of the two. He kept a moose for milking and a panther as a house pet, presumably with the permission of his wife, who had her hands full just taking care of Joe. His appetite was enormous, and the frying pan she cooked in was so big it took a side of bacon to grease it. When Joe got restless, he skated off down the Allegheny with a log raft strapped to each foot. The image of Joe with rafts on his feet no doubt arose from his real-life expertise as a lumberman, running logs and rafts on the upper Allegheny.

Mike Fink, who preferred to spell his name Miche Phinck, was "half wild horse and half cock-eyed alligator" with some "crooked snags an' red-hot snappin' turkle" thrown in. He liked to boast that he could "out-run, out-jump, out-shoot, out-brag, out-drink, an' out-fight" any man on either side of the river "from Pittsburgh to New Orleans an' back ag'in to St. Louiee." Fink didn't take kindly to the advent of the steam age and eventually, feeling the country growing too civilized, took off for the Rockies, where a murderous exploit when he was in his cups earned him a bullet through the heart.

The first steamboat on the western rivers, the *New Orleans,* was built under the supervision of Nicholas Roosevelt, a partner of Robert Fulton, in a boatyard on the north bank of the Monongahela. Launched in March 1811, the sidewheeler was greeted with "huzzas" by the townspeople but was forced because of low water to wait until October to make the trip to New Orleans. Once at New Orleans the steamer was deemed too feeble for the return trip upstream and remained on the lower Mississippi.

The first steamboats were clumsy and unwieldy, unsuited to the rivers' sometimes shallow waters and rapid currents, and their threat to the keelboat was not immediately evident. But each steamboat built brought improvements, resulting most significantly in boats of shallower draft, and in 1817 Captain Henry Shreve made the trip from New Orleans to Louisville on the steamer *Washington* in just twenty-five days. Keelboatmen had needed as much as a month just to travel the short distance from Cincinnati to Pittsburgh. Between 1812 and 1826, forty-eight steamboats were built in Pittsburgh, and as steam became preeminent, keelboatmen drifted to the rivers' tributaries or found work on the steamboats or in the yards in which they were made. One era of heroes was over. But future decades would see the germ of a new hero, and he would grow out of the story of steel.

Vessels of Fire

The first thing you notice when you enter a steel mill is the size. I had come on a snowy January morning, forty-five minutes from Pittsburgh, to visit Weirton Steel, a historic integrated steel producer, now partially owned by its employees, just over the Pennsylvania state line in Weirton, West Virginia. I had come to Weirton to get my feet wet, to bone up before the more difficult challenge of getting into the Edgar Thomson Works of U.S. Steel in the Mon Valley near Pittsburgh. I had been told mistakenly, but repeatedly, by people who seemed to have some reason to know, "You'll never get into E.T.," suggesting a secretiveness and hostility not borne out when I eventually approached them. In New York, my principal passions, apart from my job in publishing, had been the Metropolitan Opera, the Metropolitan Museum of Art, and working to improve my French. Now I had set out to learn the industrial landscape of Pittsburgh, and I knew that to know it truly I had to learn about steel.

The view on approaching the mill was of another world—the looming plant sheds, the convoluted tubing of blast furnaces, the trusswork of ore bridges over mounds of reddish ore, the winding roads through hundreds of acres of buildings large and small, metal platforms and stairs, ductwork and railroad tracks, trucks and locomotives, torpedo and thimble and other types of railroad cars. It was a scene of dazzling complexity as arcs and angles, solids and openwork, perpendiculars and bold horizontals intersected and played off one another. Shapes danced along the horizon. Monumental building walls formed solid, imposing planes. Plumes of water vapor rose from rooftops as steam issued into the cold winter air.

The steel made at Weirton is flat-rolled, "mass-produced" carbon steel, as opposed to specialty steel such as stainless, for such end-products as food and beverage cans, pipe and tube, appliances, and general packaging, and for such market sectors as steel service centers and construction. A mill like Weirton makes steel essentially as it has been made for well over a hundred years. To state it simply, iron ore is charged into a blast furnace along with coke (coal reduced in coke ovens to nearly pure carbon) and a flux of limestone to smelt molten iron. Then the molten iron is transported to a steel-making furnace to complete the transformation to steel. At newer, so-called minimills, the blast furnace process is eliminated, as steel is obtained by melting steel scrap in an electric furnace.

My reading had told me that steel is distinguished from iron primarily by its microscopic structure, but that the difference between the two has traditionally been understood most simply in terms of the amount of carbon the metal contains. The steelmaking process reduces the amount of carbon contained in pig iron from the blast furnace, making the resulting steel more malleable and ductile than cast iron, but harder and stronger than wrought iron, in which the percentage of carbon is even smaller.

Parking my car in the lot behind the Weirton City Building, I climbed into the van of the retired Weirton worker who would take the small tour group through the mill. In the seat across from me was a young clergyman who had grown up in Weirton, accompanied by his new in-laws whose accents suggested that they were Southern. As we made our way toward the mill, he leaned forward in his seat, red-and-black checked shirt under his parka, and talked animatedly, clearly eager that his in-laws understand the mill and appreciate the way of life it had defined. I suspected that behind his enthusiasm was a veil of defensiveness, an awareness that such places are often scorned. At least that's how I tend to feel in similar circumstances.

Nothing could completely prepare the uninitiated for what we were about to see. Not the exterior of the building, monumental as it was, nor any words I had read nor my knowledge of what went on inside. We descended from the van opposite the tall, rectangular portal of the BOP, the Basic Oxygen Process shop, where molten iron is transformed into steel. A wide sort of platform or bridge separated the entrance, which was several stories above ground level, from the road, and as we crossed it we looked down to see a line of torpedo cars (so called because their refractory-lined bodies resemble a torpedo) loaded with molten iron from the blast furnace. One by one the torpedo bodies would be rotated, and iron would flow out of a hole in the top into a ladle below. I have also heard them called "submarines" and "thermos cars."

Nothing had prepared me for the bedazzlement of that first moment inside, the confusion in the presence of the awesome, the momentary loss, as my dictionary phrases it, of the power to think or notice. It was as if I had entered totally without bearings the vastness of pure space. My eyes hesitated, dazed, not knowing where to land, then fixed on the towering metal wall immediately ahead. Structural details gradually came into focus, highlighted by torchlike pilot flames and the light of the furnace mouth. My gaze pushed higher and deeper into the darkness at the far end of the aisle and overhead to the trussed, corrugated roof that seemed suspended up to twenty stories above the charging floor. Gooseneck lamps shone single spots of light along the bottom chords of the trusses. Men in hard hats moved around below, rendered visibly smaller than life-size by their distance from our vantage point on the ramp, where we stood at what could be compared to choir level at the back of a cathedral. It was impossible not to feel momentarily adrift in the massive semidark.

The size of the building was commensurate with the size of the tools. The hooks of giant overhead cranes, suspended on cables, moved slowly up and down the charging aisle, with an aura of the supernatural, to lift huge trunnioned buckets, called ladles, more than eighteen feet tall, or Dumpsterlike scrap boxes loaded with metal scrap. The pear-shaped, armor-plated furnace vessel, twenty-six feet in diameter and twenty-five feet high, would be charged with molten iron and scrap totaling 425 tons. Somehow in these first moments the size of the tools only enhanced the sense of space rather than filling it. Superhuman as they were, uncontainable, literally and figuratively ungraspable, they exuded an inscrutability and indifference that made them vacant.

And yet the power of size paled in the incandescent light of molten iron and steel. I saw the basic oxygen process as a process of images: Crane hooks nestling under ladle trunnions to lift the ladle to midair above the luminous mouth of the BOP vessel, which had been pivoted on its bearings to receive the charge. Three hundred tons of molten iron poured from the ladle to the furnace in a slender stream, spraying fiery droplets against the darkness, then filling the furnace mouth with light. The iron was the consistency of milk, its color as intense as liquid sun. A lance lowered into the uprighted furnace vessel powered oxygen into the bath of molten iron and scrap at Mach 2.3, over twice the speed of sound. As carbon monoxide rose out of the bath, combining with air to form carbon dioxide, flames shot out of the gaping vessel mouth in eerie accompaniment to the rush of the oxygen blow. From charge to tap it would take forty minutes to produce a heat of steel.

Still on the ramp, we watched as the vessel pivoted forward again, the bottom rim of its mouth nearly level with the operating floor. A worker in aluminized clothing called "silvers" stood before it in the force of its incandescent glow. He reached for a long-handled metal probe with a "Popsicle" on the end, which he placed in the bath to suck up a sample of steel. One day at Edgar Thomson I would stand similarly before the furnace as heat clutched at my face, the refractory lining of the yawning furnace interior a searing yellow-white, pocked with shadows like those on the surface of the moon, a lunar landscape as hot as fire.

We stood behind the furnace as it was tapped, peering over the edge of the floor into the filling ladle, blue glasses shielding our eyes. In the blur of heat and light the teeming steel resembled the trunk of a pine, with a roiling sea at its base. I removed my glasses momentarily and felt my eyes ache with the blinding stab of light. The temperature of the steel was more than twenty-eight hundred degrees. Replacing the glasses, I stared down again, the sight hypnotic, somehow alluring, drawing me in. I could imagine leaning down, unable to resist the pull, simply diving in to dissolve into the steel. I had a sense that I was looking at the essence of the earth, at the basis of all things. I had a sense that I belonged to the steel, that it owned me, that for the first time in my life I was in the presence of the real.

It was a gut response, wholly nonrational and unbidden, a reversion to the primitive that remains part of our makeup as *Homo sapiens.* From the depths of some profound genetic predisposition came the dream of fire as the source or animator of life and the yearning to return in ecstatic, annihilating death. I found the feeling articulated in Gaston Bachelard's *Psychoanalysis of Fire,* as he speaks of the dream of destroying "the fire of our life by a superfire," of making our whole being "complete at the instant of its final ruin," the intensity of the destruction "the supreme proof, the clearest proof, of its existence," a contradiction which is "at the very root of the intuition of being."

On a transfer car the ladle moved out of view beneath us and reemerged on the opposite side of the operating floor. The turn foreman, aware that the steel was too hot, dumped a binful of cold scrap into the ladle. Because the scrap was wet, sparks flew from the molten steel in a spray that leapt over the floor rail higher than my head, then arced downward, landing at my feet. One of the givens of steelmaking is that water and molten steel do not mix. Water falling onto steel will erupt as steam. Molten steel poured onto water will explode, violently, as water trapped by the steel turns to steam and powers its escape. Glenn McIntyre, the turn foreman, stopped to chat with us. As he spoke, he took a Baby Ruth bar from his pocket and peeled off the wrapper, crumpling it into a ball and tossing it into the scrap bin. I was scandalized at the thought that the wrapper would eventually find its way into a ladle, and at what I took to be Mac's willingness to sully the steel, until I stopped to remember that at twenty-eight-hundred-plus degrees, the wrapper would for all intents and purposes simply cease to exist.

The smelting and processing of molten metal—iron and steel—is the most otherworldly aspect of a steel mill, the most susceptible to metaphor, the element that speaks most directly to the metaphysical imagination. Even common parlance suggests a multiplicity of associations. Writers have referred repeatedly to Dante in the face of cauldronlike vessels and fire. Under soaring roofs observers think of the lofty spaces of cathedrals. The workers themselves are not immune. During one of my visits to Edgar Thomson, Manny Stoupis, the burly blast furnace process manager, recalled Dorothy Six, once the largest blast furnace in the area. "Big Dorothy," he called her. "A hell of a lady." A blast furnace is female for obvious reasons. She is charged with ore, then the ore is transformed in the fire of her voluminous belly. At the moment of birth molten iron bursts from her taphole amid a shower of sparks and light. "A blast furnace is temperamental as a woman," Manny said. "You feed her wrong, she gets constipated. You gotta treat 'em well." At this point I began to think I'd heard all I wanted of the analogy. "You get to know blast furnaces like women's bodies," he said.

Molten steel takes its first solid form at Weirton in a continuous slab caster, a complex of rolls shaped like a ski jump, topped by a rectangular, open-bottomed mold into which the molten steel is poured. Already in the mold the steel is assuming its rectangular shape, forming an outer shell around the still liquid interior. The strand of steel tries to explode apart as it is extruded into then driven through the rolls, which resemble giant washing machine wringers maintaining the steel's shape. Emerging into the cutting zone, the now completely solid strand is cut by an acetylene torch into slabs up to forty-nine inches wide, four hundred inches (33.3 feet) long, and nine inches thick, weighing as much as twenty tons. Later, the slabs will be transported to the rolling mills where they will be rolled to a gauge as thin as five-thousandths of an inch. In the past, molten steel from the steelmaking furnace was teemed into ingot molds to make ingots, which after cooling and re-heating were rolled into slabs or other shapes. The continuous caster refined the process to produce slabs or other shapes in a single step.

Later, at the caster at E.T., dressed in silvers, I would stand on a platform at CP-3 (Control Panel 3) with the bottom of the ladle at eye level. The ladle sat on a turret, poised over a tundish, the huge bathtub-shaped vessel that would control the flow of steel into the caster's mold. Even the buttons on the control panel were outsized, like large thread spools. I pressed the button indicated by the assistant strand operator and activated the robot arm, which swung around to find the nozzle on the ladle's bottom, then lifted a refractory shroud around it to protect the steel from the air. I pressed another button, and the ladle began to lower, then another to open the nozzle's slidegate. Steel poured into the tundish. I was in awe really of the weight and the forces I had set into motion, and had been tense with the fear of doing something wrong. I had imagined losing control of the ladle, spilling a sea of molten steel.

Again the tools were gigantic. So much in a steel mill exceeds our intellectual grasp. What does a temperature of 2,800 degrees even mean when the boiling point of water is 212, and seems plenty hot at that? How heavy is 300 tons, 600,000 pounds? What does it feel like to lift it? How do you imagine the strength that can squeeze solid steel?

I saw one of Weirton's two blast furnaces on another day,

out in the open, over two hundred feet high, with its crown of bulbous, convoluted ductwork. Skip cars climbed the skip bridge to the hopper at the top of the furnace with coke, ore, and flux. The area around the furnace was a complex network of bins, tracks, platforms, wall-less floors, tread-patterned walkways and steps. As I stood close by on the cast floor, blue flames of escaping gas licked up the furnace's side. I had to shout over the furnace's roar.

The blast of natural gas and heated air entered the furnace through tuyeres (pronounced *tweers*) linked to the huge bustle pipe that circled the bosh. Through a peep sight in the tuyere cap I could see the searing yellow white of the conflagration inside. As the burden descended, supported and fired from below by the blast, melted iron drained to the hearth. Flux combined with impurities in the ore to form slag, which accumulated on top of the iron. Rounding the furnace, I could see the taphole at hearth level, packed hard and tight with dirty, off-white clay.

Every two hours the furnace is tapped. As the moment for tapping approached, runners leading from the trough below the taphole filled with flame as natural gas was piped in to heat them before the cast. From a glass-enclosed control station the team leader directed an automated drill into the clay-packed taphole, five or more feet, then withdrew it, its bore red orange. Liquid iron spilled forth. The area swelled with light. Sparks the size of a child's fist burst from the taphole and up from the iron runner. Cinder snappers dressed in silvers stood alongside, plunging long poles through the crust of cooling iron that began to form over the flowing metal, pulling them out aflame. Iron poured over the edge of the floor into a torpedo car below on its track, sparks and flames bursting from its mouth as the iron flowed. This was pig iron on its way to the BOP to become steel. Once the iron was tapped, molten slag, as luminous as the iron, would be channeled through its runner toward the opposite edge of the floor, where it would flow over the edge into thimble cars.

Even today a steel mill, largely automated as it is, is dangerous, in spite of significant efforts, particularly in unionized mills, to keep the workplace safe. Accidents range from the trivial to the fatal and their occasional, apparent flukiness only underscores the fact that, as human frailty operates in an arena this complex, events can come together in an unforeseen and probably infinite variety of ways. Over the past few years I have read dozens of accident reports, most of them of accidents, here and elsewhere, that were not serious: sprains, splinters, minor burns, lacerations, abrasions, and contusions. There was even the worker who bought a hot dog from a vending machine and, trying to tear off the plastic wrapper, broke his tooth.

Far less often the accidents are more serious, even grisly, as workers are burned, crushed, electrocuted, or killed in explosions. Reports for recent years include several incidents of molten metal spilling from ladles or BOP vessels, engulfing workers in radiant heat and flames. Human skin splashed by steel comes away in sheets at the touch of a hand. I have also seen a report of a worker caught in an explosion as molten steel broke out of a furnace and mixed with water from a line damaged in the breakout. Another report tells of a coiler operator in the tin mill (a finishing mill in which rolled steel is coated with tin) thought to have been caught by the rolls and pulled into the moving strip of steel. A friend of mine who worked at the plant tells me that the woman's leg was cut off, her body nearly cut in half, and her skull crushed.

Early iron and steelmaking was even more difficult and dangerous than it is today. Until automatic skip-hoist systems were installed, workers called "top fillers" dumped materials into the hopper at the top of a blast furnace by hand, prey to poisonous gas and the possibility of explosion, in temperatures of up to 130 degrees. Puddlers, among the most skilled of metalworkers, worked molten pig iron, refining it to malleable iron, in a puddling furnace by manipulating a long, twenty-five-pound rod called a "rabble" through the furnace door. A contemporary photograph by Lewis Hine shows a puddler at work, bent toward the furnace, arms extended to manipulate the rabble, face and body aglow in the hot metal light. It was arduous work, stirring and mixing the metal boil as it began to thicken, working the solidifying mass into balls and maneuvering it from the furnace. James Davis, a Welsh immigrant who arrived in the "new country" in 1881 at the age of eight, wrote of his time as a puddler, of "half-naked, soot-smeared fellows [fighting] the furnace hearths with hooks, rabbles and paddles," their "scowling faces . . . lit with fire," sweat pouring over their arms and backs.

Workers once charged open hearth furnaces—long used in this country but now supplanted by the BOP—by hand, feeding red-hot pig iron hammered into pieces into the furnace with a flattened iron bar called a "peel." Even with the advent of charging machines, workers had to add refractory materials, for temporary relining, by hand. Charles Rumford Walker recalled the procedure in *Steel: The Diary of a Furnace Worker*: "All the men on the furnace and all the men on your neighbor's furnace form a dolomite line, and marching in file to the open door, fling their shovelfuls across the flaming void to the back-wall. It's not a beginner's job. You must swing your weapon through a wide arc, to give it 'wing.'" Elaborating on the technique, he continued, "The mouth of the furnace gapes its widest, and you must hug close in order to get the stuff

44

across. Every man has deeply smoked glasses on his nose when he faces the furnace. He's got to stare down her throat, to watch where the dolomite lands." He offers some advice: "Throw your left arm high at the end of your arc, and in front of your face; it will cut the heat an instant, and allow you to see if you have 'placed' without flinching. It's really not brawn . . . but a nimble swing and a good eye, and the art of not minding heat."

I had a look firsthand at an early rolling process, still being used at Braeburn Alloy Steel (up the Allegheny from Pittsburgh), in which the work on the rolling mills is done by hand. The company works with exotic metals, rolling small lots in small quantities, doing jobs that are not economical for the bigger mills. On the morning I arrived, I was met by Brad Huwar, one of the managers, a rugged, handsome man, dark-haired and impeccably polite, who led me along the somewhat circuitous route from the main office to the rolling mill. As we walked, he explained that the company had once been a high-speed tool producer, but as the business became more unprofitable the company had turned to conversion, processing metal sent to them by other companies and then returning it. One of their specialties now is rolling Titanium 6-4 ELI, to be forged or machined into shapes for medical implants. As opposed to the bigger mills, Braeburn is paid by the pound not by the ton.

The temperature was nine degrees that morning and seemed little warmer inside the vast, high-ceilinged building that housed the rolling mills, which seemed diminutive in comparison. The men clustered around cylindrical gas-fed heaters, called salamanders, during their breaks, as the only other source of warmth was the sun-colored metal bars they would feed into the rolls. Away from the salamanders, as Brad showed

45

me the roll stands, my hands began to stiffen, making it difficult to write, and my ballpoint pen was no help, as the ink barely flowed in the cold. My notes were palely colored indentations in the paper.

The company has two sets of roll stands, the 14-inch mill and the 10-inch mill, each arranged in a single, fencelike line. The men were working the 14-inch mill on the day I was there (so called because the diameter of the rolls is fourteen inches), rolling four-inch square bars of Alloy 9310, seventeen inches long, into flats measuring five-eighths by three inches by twelve feet long. Each stand had three rolls, except for the finishing stand which had two, and six men were working, three on each side. The men passed the bar back and forth, first through the upper rolls, then back through the lower, moving from one stand to the next, from roughing to step rolls to flattening and edging to finishing. With each pass, the rolls reduced the size of the bar, flattening, edging, lengthening, until, with the final pass, the finishing rolls removed the warp and sent the flat forth in its final dimension, straight and true. I asked Brad how much the bars weighed.

"These bars weigh seventy-six pounds," he said. "But we work with bars of up to 250 pounds."

At times the rolling process had the rhythm and sweep of a dance, as the men sent the luminous, reheated bars back and forth through the rolls with tongs and a long hook hanging from a monorail above. The occasional arclike sweep as a worker drew the lengthening strip from the rolls then returned it was as beautiful in line and movement as anything I have ever seen, and seemed all the more impressive given the weight the men were manipulating.

During a break the men returned to the heater. Brad introduced me to Rich Verner, the roller in charge, a pleasant man with graying hair, who has spent thirty-two years in the mill. He is proud of the mill and the wealth of knowledge he has gained there. "I tell my workers they have only ten years till I retire," he said. "Ten years to learn the ins and outs of the job."

He worries that the younger workers seem unwilling to learn and take responsibility and wonders how he is going to be able to pass his knowledge on. "You need special people here," he said. "Mechanically inclined, willing to work hard, stand up to the heat of summer." I couldn't help but think of the cold of winter.

The men work one heat; that is, they roll the contents of one batch-type reheat furnace, then break for fifteen minutes. Human muscle could bear little more. The work is hard. And dangerous. Guides on the roll housings or the bars themselves may fly out, hitting and burning nearby workers. At one time there was an electric furnace in the melt shop at the far end of the building, charged by hand with scrap, turnings, old tools, whatever. Smoke billowed out of the melt shop toward the roll stands.

"During a sulfur heat," Rich told me, "we'd just start choking and have to go outside."

People have invested so much in this place, have given themselves so intensely to it. I think particularly of members of the great wave of immigration that began toward the end of the last century. Between 1880 and 1914, millions of immigrants from eastern and southern Europe headed for Pittsburgh and other American cities to find work in the country's burgeoning industries. Some intended to settle here, others to return to the old country once they had saved enough for modest comfort in a radically changing Europe. Entering Pittsburgh's heavy industries in greatest numbers were Italians and so-called Slavs: Poles, Slovaks, Ukrainians, Hungarians, Croatians, Carpatho-Rusyns, Serbians, Slovenes, and others, ethnically distinct but little differentiated in the American public mind. Some, such as the Hungarians, or Magyars, were not Slavic at all.

Eastern European immigrants, whose early years in the Pittsburgh area are particularly well documented, voiced their dream in the Slovak expression *za chlebom,* or its equivalent in their own language, meaning literally "going for bread." Largely unskilled, their languages unintelligible to the previous, predominantly northern European immigrant groups that held the more skilled positions in the mills, these "Slavs," or "Hunkies," as they were disparagingly called (the word *Hunky* is believed to be a shortened, altered version of the word *Hungarian;* a large percentage of these immigrants were members of ethnic minorities belonging to the Austro-Hungarian Empire), these "Slavs" were given the hardest, hottest, and dirtiest jobs, and after a day's or night's work went home to neighborhoods in which living conditions were abysmal.

Margaret Byington offers a telling description of a "Slavic" court in *Homestead: The Households of a Mill Town,* published in 1910 as part of the Pittsburgh Survey, a landmark study of urban social conditions funded by the Russell Sage Foundation. (The Pittsburgh area was chosen not because it was exceptional but because it was representative of American industrial life.) Located behind the dark sheds and stacks of Carnegie Steel, which stood between the neighborhood and the river, the courtyard Byington describes is small, bordered on three sides by the backs of "smoke-grimed" frame houses, on the fourth by stables. "Children, dogs and hens make it lively under foot," she writes. "Overhead long lines of flapping clothes must be dodged. A group of women stand gossiping in one corner, awaiting their turn at the pump,—which is one of the two sources of water supply for the 20 families who live here. Another woman dumps the contents of her washtubs upon the paved ground, and the greasy, soapy water runs into an open drain a few feet from the pump." The image becomes fuller when we think of how women dressed in that period— the blouses and billowing, floor-length skirts. "In the center," Byington continues, "a circular wooden building with ten compartments opening into one vault, flushed only by this waste water, constitutes the toilet accommodations for over one hundred people."

Some families lived four or five to a tenement room. Children had to be shushed by their mothers or sent outside as fathers on night turn slept. To augment the household's wages, many took in boarders, single men without families or married men who had left wives and children at home. It was not uncommon for boarders in lodging houses to share a bed with others working different shifts, crawling into a bed still warm from the body that had preceded it. Infant mortality was high: statistics show that in 1907, for every three "Slavic" children born, one child under the age of two died.

In the year 1907–1908, nearly 80 percent of steel mill workers worked twelve-hour days. One out of five worked seven-day weeks. Men returned home from the mill grimy and exhausted, with time for little more than sleep. Every second week came the infamous twenty-four-hour "long turn," as seven-day men, who had worked the previous week on day shift, worked from Sunday morning until Monday morning so as to switch from day turn to night. Many turned to the taverns that lined the streets near the mills, for companionship and to relieve the burden of their work. Portraits drawn by Joseph Stella for the Pittsburgh Survey give an eloquent and haunting identity to these largely anonymous men. A hatted worker with hollow eyes stares at the viewer, hands gripping his tongs, as ingot light and shadow play over his sturdy face. A young "day laborer" looks hard to the viewer's right, hair tousled, with creases between his heavy brows, his mouth set in a look of defiant strength. An "old Slav" looks gratefully, his head slightly tilted, at the bread he holds delicately in his long-fingered hand.

The work of the mill laborer's wife was as arduous as her husband's: preparing meals, cleaning house, washing, ironing, sewing, baking, shopping, mending for family and boarders, continually interrupted by children and the varying work schedules of the men. S. J. Kleinberg describes a typical washday in *The Shadow of the Mills*, her book about working-class families in Pittsburgh from 1870 to 1907: "Working-class women did laundry the old-fashioned way. They brought water in from the pump, heated it on a coal or wood stove, emptied it into a washtub, and scrubbed the clothes as they bent over the 'back-breaking washboard.' They carried the soapy water outside, brought clean water in, heated it again, and rinsed the clothes. Especially sweaty or dirty clothes, those worn by men in the mills or children's play clothes and soiled infant wear, were soaped and rinsed again, then wrung out and hung out to dry in the courtyard, alleyway, or kitchen." The washing took all day. As evening approached the woman would tidy herself and her children for her husband's return and prepare the evening meal. It was the woman who held the family together, who set the tone for domestic life, and whose degree of managerial ability—to budget, to choose food wisely, to get her work done—largely determined the family's degree of comfort.

Throughout the Pittsburgh district, working-class housing clung to pieces of land not wanted by the mills, prey to their din and the grit-filled black smoke that belched from their stacks. Kleinberg writes of an Italian woman living in a "back house" added to an already existing building, "a ten-by-six cubicle with a two-foot-square window directly opposite and two feet from the privy's door." She also notes the poor housing conditions for African Americans and the remark by one African-American worker that the "only place where there is plenty of room for Negroes is in the alleys." In 1915, in a typical "foreign-speaking" settlement in the Strip District, forty-three industrial families lived in the shadow of Crucible Steel, in an area covering half a block. Thirty-two of them kept a total of 169 boarders, or more than five boarders per family. Land nearby, given to the city for use as a park, was bare earth stacked with old pipe.

The laborer's lack of power was nowhere more evident than in the rapidly changing iron and steel industries, and above all in the corporate empires of Andrew Carnegie and Henry Clay Frick. Andrew Carnegie (pronounced *Car-nay'-gie*) was born in 1836 in Dunfermline, Scotland, to William Carnegie, a handloom weaver and Chartist, and his wife Margaret, herself the daughter of a longtime political radical. He emigrated to Pittsburgh with his family in 1848, after the mechanization of the textile industry forced his father out of work, and began his meteoric rise as messenger then operator for a telegraph company. His enterprise and common sense soon attracted the notice of Thomas Scott, superintendent of the Western Division of the Pennsylvania Railroad, who hired him away as his personal operator and private secretary. It was probably at Scott's request that Carnegie, at twenty-two, was included among the investors—along with Scott himself and J. Edgar Thomson, the railroad's president—in the Woodruff Sleeping

Car Company, an investment that would become the germ of Carnegie's fortune. The three men would continue as investment partners in a variety of railroading and bridge-building ventures, until Carnegie's refusal to endanger his other holdings by endorsing Scott's notes during the panic of 1873 led to a break with Scott and some strain in the relationship with Thomson. In an attempt to assure the goodwill of the Pennsylvania, Carnegie promptly named his first major steel mill for Thomson, the Edgar Thomson Steel Works in Braddock, or as it has been called from the beginning, E.T. Not surprisingly, the plant named for the railroad's president was built to produce rails.

The five-foot three-inch corporate titan was a consummate businessman, an astute judge of managerial talent, who operated on a fundamental principle: Watch the costs, and the profits will take care of themselves. The Carnegie mills were at the forefront worldwide in layout, design, and technology, and Carnegie thought nothing of scrapping even new equipment if a more efficient process came along. He was also a master negotiator, cobbling a group of companies—coal and coke, ore fields, railroads—to his primary holdings to ensure control of every element of the steelmaking process from raw material to finished product, a concept referred to as vertical integration.

Carnegie's alliance with Henry Clay Frick would provide a crucial element of large-scale steelmaking: ample and economical supplies of coke. Frick was the son of John Frick, a modest farmer, but grandson of Abraham Overholt, a farmer and distiller of rye whiskey, and one of the wealthiest men in Westmoreland County (the county to Allegheny's east). Frick had made a fortune out of "cinder," the bituminous coal that farmers of the area used for domestic purposes but otherwise regarded as little more than an obstruction to their plows. Staking his future, and his vow to become twice as rich as his grandfather, who was his childhood hero, Frick joined a cousin's floundering coking operation, and rather than liquidating the company's holdings, borrowed $52,995 to expand them. Nor did he stop there. Borrowing from members of his family, and on the legacy he would someday receive from his grandparents, as well as that of his mother and sister, he quietly and obsessively pursued his dream of coke, acquiring more coal lands and building more dome-shaped, "beehive" ovens, turning finally to Judge Thomas Mellon, the banker, for additional loans when his other sources ran dry. By his thirtieth birthday in 1879, he had accumulated his first million and had fulfilled his childhood vow.

And still he pushed. "More coal, more ovens," wrote Carnegie's biographer Joseph Frazier Wall, "more freight cars and barges to move the coke to the mills—this had become the only meaningful rhythm of his life." Coal tipples, coke ovens, company "patch" towns with their rows of identical frame houses proliferated over the landscape of the Connellsville region, named for the town fifty miles southeast of Pittsburgh. Smoke and cinders spewed out of the ovens, spreading over the nearby houses, dirtying rugs and curtains, even the vegetables and flowers in family gardens. The air filled with the smell of burning coal. The beehive ovens were shaped like igloos, or beehives, made of brick and were often built in a single line of up to one hundred or more into a bank or the side of a hill. (Ovens were also often seen joined back to back in free-standing double rows.) Coal was charged through a hole in the roof called a "trunnel-head," and was burned with very little air over a period of forty-eight to seventy-two hours to remove the more volatile matter. Then the burning mass was quenched with water, leaving the nearly pure carbon, or coke, which was "pulled" or "drawn" from the furnace out of a door in the furnace's front wall. At the industry's height, forty-four thousand beehive ovens operated in the Connellsville region, site of the best coking coal in the world.

Leo "Bud" Shearer worked for seventeen years in the Frick-owned coke ovens at Mammoth in southern Westmoreland County until the site was closed down in 1959. (By World War I coke making was shifting to huge "by-product" coke plants which recover the escaping volatile elements—tar, oils, ammonia, and gas—for further use, but the more primitive beehive process survived into the 1960s and beyond. The country's last commercial beehive operation closed down in 1983.) Bud and his wife Sue sat with me in their kitchen at their farm in Donegal Township, at the big, rectangular table Bud had made himself years before.

"I tended four ovens," he said, "and pulled two a day. First you pulled the bricks out of the door with a hook and laid them to the side, and then you hosed down the coke. Then you used a scraper to break up the coke and pull it."

A scraper is an eighteen-foot rod, with a twenty-inch blade on one end, like a hoe, that went into the oven on a pulley hung in the open door. The other end of the rod formed a T, one side of which the puller hooked around his backside. With the scraper head lodged in the coke, the worker rocked repeatedly against the T end to pry the coke apart, then with the rod in his hands pulled the coke toward the oven door.

"You'd shovel the coke with a coke fork into a wheelbarrow and wheel it up a ramp to a railway car," Bud said. The coke came out in chunks, silvery gray and porous, much lighter than an equivalent piece of coal.

Once the coke was removed, the puller bricked up the

door halfway. The oven would be charged again and a worker called a "leveler" would use a smaller scraper to distribute the coal evenly before bricking up the top half of the door. Ten tons of coal would be charged for a forty-eight-hour burn.

"I'd go to work about three in the morning," Bud said, "and usually finished about eleven."

"He'd come home black," Sue recalled, "and exhausted. He'd lie down on the couch and go to sleep and the kids would crawl all over him and he wouldn't even know they were there."

"At night you saw rows of fires all over the countryside," Bud said, referring to the flames issuing from the trunnel heads. "You could see them for miles."

The first meeting of Andrew Carnegie and Henry Clay Frick is described by Joseph Frazier Wall. Frick had by this time allowed himself the distraction of marrying. On his honeymoon trip to New York and Washington he was invited to dinner by Carnegie, who was one of his best customers but whom he had never met. Suspecting that Carnegie was up to something, but not knowing what, Frick sat stonily through the dinner and the toasts to the new couple. Carnegie was at his most charming. Then his designs became clear as he raised his glass again, this time to the Frick-Carnegie partnership, which he treated as a fait accompli, though no more than a few discreet feelers had taken place. By the time of that dinner in 1881, Frick controlled 80 percent of the coalfields and coke ovens of the Connellsville region and could well see the advantages to himself in such an alliance. Within a month Carnegie and his associates had bought a minority interest in the Henry C. Frick Coke Company. Within two years, they had bought up over 50 percent. Beyond the immediate infusion of capital, further benefits would accrue to Frick, whom Carnegie valued as much for his managerial talent as for his coke. In 1887 Frick became a minority owner in Carnegie Brothers & Company and in January 1889 was appointed the company's chairman.

Economic recession and labor unrest were to play significant roles in Carnegie's acquisition of two newly built competitors, the Pittsburg Bessemer Steel Company at Homestead, which he quickly adapted to the production of beams and then expanded to produce armor plate, and the Allegheny Bessemer Works in Duquesne, whose acquisition provided a classic example of business dirty tricks. The plant at Duquesne was rolling ingots directly from furnaces called "soaking pits" without the additional cooling and reheating that was the accepted practice at the time. Alarmed at the competitive advantage in eliminating one expensive step, Carnegie circulated a notice to the railroads even before the start-up of the plant warning that its rails would be defective because they would lack the necessary "homogeneity" of structure. Faced with the supposed doubts of so prominent a steel man as Carnegie, the market for the rails naturally suffered. Needless to say, once Carnegie had acquired the mill, direct rolling was not only retained at Duquesne, but was adopted at Homestead and E.T as well.

On July 1, 1892, the Carnegie holdings—which included the Edgar Thomson, Homestead, Duquesne, and Hartman steel works, the Upper and Lower Union Mills, the Lucy Furnaces (named for Carnegie's sister-in-law Lucy Coleman Carnegie), the Keystone Bridge Works, the Scotia mines, and the Larimer and Youghiogeny coke works—were consolidated, largely through the efforts of Henry Clay Frick, who was subsequently elected its chairman, in a single company called the Carnegie Steel Company, Limited. It was the world's largest steel company, with a capacity of over half the steel production of Great

Britain. The Homestead Works alone had thirty-seven acres "under roof."

Wrought iron was giving way to steel, which was metallurgically superior for such products as structural shapes and rails, and which, with the invention of the Bessemer converter, such as those installed at E.T., and the development of the open hearth, which would predominate at Homestead, could now be mass-produced. Technological innovation made production far less dependent on the speed and skill of particular individuals. An open hearth could produce twenty-five tons in one heat, a puddler up to five hundred pounds. Material handling was increasingly mechanized with such developments as automatic roller tables, changing the type of worker required. Puddlers and rollers had operated as independent contractors in the mills. Now their skills were becoming an anachronism in large-scale production. Many smaller iron and steel companies survived in the Pittsburgh area, successfully exploiting specialized market niches that did not compete directly with the Carnegie mills. In many of these mills the skills of the puddler, among others, were still required. But the area of real growth was represented by Carnegie. The massive changes exemplified in Carnegie's mills in method and scale of production are often referred to as the second industrial revolution.

The year that marked the consolidation of the Carnegie holdings also marked a landmark in labor history. On June 29, 1892, two days before the merger took effect, Frick shut down the Homestead Works. His target was the Amalgamated Association of Iron and Steel Workers, a craft union of skilled workers that Carnegie and Frick, in their relentless pursuit of the lowest possible production costs and unquestioned control of the steelmaking process, were no longer willing to tolerate.

(Carnegie and Frick gained strength from the fact that the skills of the union members were becoming less relevant to their operations.) Homestead was the last of the company's holdings in which the union had a significant presence. At the end of April, Carnegie was on his way to his annual sojourn in Scotland, which left Frick to break the union and, conveniently, for the sake of Carnegie's image, to bear the responsibility, which Frick was more than happy to do. Carnegie, after all, was on record, in an article written for *Forum* magazine in 1886, as being opposed to strikebreaking: "To expect that one dependent upon his daily wage for the necessaries of life will stand peaceably and see a new man employed in his stead is to expect much," he wrote. "There is an unwritten law among the best workmen: 'Thou shalt not take thy neighbor's job.'" (It should be noted that shortly thereafter, during the lockout at Edgar Thomson of 1888, Carnegie brought in Pinkertons to protect nonunion workers, ultimately defeating unionism at the plant.) Carnegie would spend much of his life trying to reconcile his compulsion to get ahead with the idealism of his father and his grandfather, to reconcile his business practices with his desire to be, in the words of historian Paul Krause, a kind employer—and a good man. Frick was no doubt pleased to have him out of the picture. The two did not entirely agree on strategy. Carnegie preferred simply to post a notice declaring that unionism was to end. Frick's approach would be more devious. But Carnegie's note to Frick after his departure gave Frick all the leeway he needed: "We all approve of anything you do," Carnegie wrote, "not stopping short of approval of a contest. We are with you to the end." The consensus of historians is that Carnegie did not anticipate the bloodiness of the contest to come.

It would be difficult to say the same for Frick, who pretended to bargain in good faith while demanding concessions that would ultimately lead to wage reductions not only for members of the Amalgamated but for all but the least skilled workers. When the Amalgamated declined to meet Frick's deadline for accepting a new contract as a union, Frick ended all negotiations and completed the erection of an eleven-foot, solid plank fence around the mill, topped with barbed wire, to protect it from assault. The fence was perforated at intervals "as if for the convenience of sharpshooters," and platforms twelve feet high, armed with searchlights, were erected near the mill buildings. Townspeople would dub the fortification "Fort Frick." On June 25, the company announced that it would negotiate only with individual workers and not with the Amalgamated. On the same day, Frick wrote to the Pinkerton National Detective Agency, asking for three hundred Pinkerton guards to be dispatched to Homestead on July 5. On June 28, the company closed the 119-inch plate mill and one of the open hearth departments. That night, workers hanged Frick and the mill's superintendent John Potter in effigy. On June 29, the company locked all thirty-eight hundred workers out of the mill, and the entire mill was closed down. Fearing correctly that Frick would import strikebreakers and the hated Pinkertons, as he had done previously in the coke fields, the nearly four thousand workers mobilized to watch the mill twenty-four hours a day. Frick fired them all and declared the mill nonunion.

What followed, in the workers' view, was a battle for individual liberty, for what they believed to be the fundamental principle of American democracy. "The constitution of this country guarantees all men the right to live," declared John McLuckie, a skilled worker and burgess of Homestead, "but in order to live we must keep up a continuous struggle." Workers believed that their labor had a value in and of itself, and that it entitled them to a minimum fair wage, unrelated to the ups and downs of the market. At 4:30 A.M. on July 6, barges carrying over three hundred Pinkertons landed at the mill site, to be confronted by a major portion of the population of the town. No one knows for sure who, in the confusion, fired the first shot, but by evening seven workers and/or sympathizers and three Pinkertons had been killed.

It was a day of passion and ineptitude. A cannon, borrowed from the courthouse square and charged with dynamite, blew up when the charge was lighted. Townspeople concocted repeated strategies to set the barges on fire, without success. One intrepid group piled a raft with oil-soaked lumber, set it on fire, then propelled the raft downriver. The flames died before the raft reached its target. Henry Striegel, a sympathizer, shot himself by accident with his own gun, then succumbed to fire from the barges as he lay in the mill yard. Steelworker Silas Wain was a victim of friendly fire. Still, the Pinkertons were far outnumbered; morale on the barges was low, and many had been reluctant to fight to begin with. With the intervention of William Weihe, president of the Amalgamated, and union president-elect M. M. Garland, among others, strike leaders were persuaded to let the Pinkertons surrender. They were unable to ensure the Pinkertons' safety, however, and the hapless men were forced to run a gauntlet of jeering townspeople armed with clubs and stones.

In spite of the surrender, the Homestead Strike would ultimately end in the defeat of unionism at Homestead. Government forces weighed in on the side of Carnegie and Frick as eight thousand National Guard troops were ordered to Homestead to police the reopening of the mill. Even public opinion, which had largely supported the workers, wavered in the face of the assassination attempt on Frick's life by a twenty-three-year-old anarchist, Alexander Berkman, a Russian Jewish immigrant connected with Emma Goldman. On the day after the shooting the *New York Times* reported that Berkman, who was not connected with the Amalgamated, "believed in murdering capitalists who should refuse to give up their property," and had vowed to shoot down any employer who refused to yield to the demands of his employees. But the assassination attempt did nothing to lessen Frick's resolve. The company would win by attrition as replacement workers took over the strikers' jobs.

In 1901, a merger put together by J. P. Morgan created the United States Steel Corporation, the world's first billion-dollar corporation. The price of the Carnegie company's holdings represented nearly half of that total: $480 million. Carnegie, who fancied himself a political and social philosopher as well as a businessman, and who read and published voluminously on a variety of topics, would now turn more fully to the business of "constructive" philanthropy, epitomized by the establishment of the libraries that bear his name. Carnegie considered himself an agent of progress, and much of his philanthropy was a testament to his faith in "useful knowledge." It was also somewhat presumptuous and self-serving.

Accepting that the laws of evolutionary biology would inevitably lead to the concentration of wealth in the hands of the few, Carnegie espoused a philanthropy that would, in the words of historian Roy Lubove, "provide the ladders upon which the deserving could rise." The rich man was simply a trustee of his wealth, which should be used for the common good. (It was, of course, up to the rich man to determine what the common good was.) Part of Carnegie, the ruthless "robber baron," wanted to be, indeed considered himself, the working man's friend. He had grown up, after all, in a family acutely conscious of working men's rights, and he had experienced poverty himself. (He also fully enjoyed the adulation his philanthropies brought.) Over the entrance to the main branch of the Carnegie Library of Pittsburgh is the legend "Free to the People." But it was also "the people" who paid. In the words of the *Commoner,* quoted in the *New York World* in 1892, "The money which has gone to the erection of the structures which he presents represents so much money taken away from the men who really earned it." Carnegie accepted that not every individual would come out ahead in his grand scheme.

In 1901, a member of the executive committee of the newly formed U.S. Steel Corporation remarked, "I have always had one rule. If a workman sticks up his head, hit it." Carnegie and Frick had conspired in the defeat of the union. Union leaders at Homestead had been blacklisted from the steel industry for life. Subsequent strikes in 1901 and 1909 eliminated any pockets of unionism that remained at U.S. Steel. Other mills followed the Carnegie company's lead. John N. Ingham points out in *Making Iron and Steel* that more tolerance of unionism was shown in many of the smaller mills. But by 1900 no steel mill of any importance in western Pennsylvania recognized the union. Not until the 1930s, when the federal government made collective bargaining mandatory, would the working man begin to have an official voice in the mill.

It was the circumstances of this world that gave birth to Joe Magarac, the biggest, tallest, prettiest steelworker of them all. Of undifferentiated "Slavic" extraction and at least seven feet tall, Joe had a back as big as a door, a neck like a bull's, and, in Irwin Shapiro's account, wore "Size 18 extra-special wide-last triple-soled safety-toe shoes." He was a born steelman who worked both night turn and day turn seven days a week, and was in fact made of steel, dining on "hot steel soup" and "old ingots for meat." A spirited, cheerful giant who loved to work, he appeared among ordinary laborers in moments of dire emergency and effortlessly saved their lives. William Gropper's well-known painting of 1946 depicts an ebullient, muscled Joe looming in the foreground, bending a red-hot bar of steel in hot steel hands. The bar's arc is echoed in the background by the curving blast furnace downcomer. Here was a man as strong as a machine, an industrial hero for a hot-metal age. In dying, he returned to the stuff of which he was made, jumping into a ladle and melting into the molten steel, ultimately to be rolled into beams and channels for a new mill, the finest mill that ever was.

There is some dispute over the origins of the Magarac legend. Tradition has it that the legend grew up among immigrant workers in Braddock in the 1870s. There is also persuasive evidence that Magarac-type stories circulated at Pittsburgh Steel in Monessen after the turn of the century. But there is no question that the legend was significantly embellished on Joe's first appearance in print, in a story by a former Mon Valley steelworker published in *American Mercury* in 1929. (Some scholars believe that this story is the legend's true origin.) But whatever its origins, it is undeniable that the figure of Joe Magarac is a telling embodiment of the power, the danger, and the superhuman aura of steelmaking, and a major element of its folklore.

For the year 1906–1907, Pittsburgh Survey author John Fitch cited 195 fatalities in the steel plants of the Pittsburgh district. More than half were caused by conditions common to all heavy manufacturing, and so were mirrored in other industries. "Industrial railroads and traveling cranes are common in all large construction companies," wrote Crystal Eastman in another volume of the Survey, "in almost all factories there is repair work, cleaning, oiling, etc., to be done at a dangerous height." Women and children were not immune. Cork making, the garment trades, hinge making, laundry work—in these and other industries that employed women and children, there was always the danger of injury. Hands and arms could be crushed in a mangle, fingers cut off by punching machines. Brass dust filled the air of lamp factories. In 1862, seventy-nine people, mostly young girls aged fourteen and fifteen, were killed in an explosion at the Allegheny Arsenal, a manufacturer of munitions for the Union Army.

But it was the furnaces above all that seized the imagination, that became the grisliest motif in the folklore of the steelworker's world. After an explosion, women and children and men working other shifts rushed to the mill to learn the fate of their co-workers, husbands, and sons. The image is more familiar to us in the context of coal mines. Workers and their families have been haunted by the image of the worker dissolving into molten iron and steel. In *Steel: The Diary of a Furnace Worker,* published in 1922, John Rumford Walker recalls being told of molten steel breaking out of a Bessemer converter, catching twenty-four men in the flow. "The company," the story goes, "with a sense of the proprieties, waited until the families of the men moved [away] before putting the scrap, which contained them, back into the furnace for re-melting." Mary Heaton Vorse, author of *Men and Steel,* was told of "a man made into iron rails, of another who went into the structure of great buildings."

In *Crisis in Bethlehem,* published in 1986, John Strohmeyer recalls hearing of a worker on the open hearth "who slipped and vanished into a ladle of hot steel. When no remnant of the victim could be retrieved, the company reportedly buried the entire ladle at the cinder dump." He quotes a steelworker speaking on mill conditions in the 1950s and his account of another worker who was blown into the ladle as a heat of steel was tapped. "You would think," he said, "that the human body would melt immediately, you know, the steel is bubbling at about twenty-nine hundred degrees Fahrenheit. But frankly things don't melt that easily. They told me that the heels and the safety helmet floated for some time afterward." A couple of years ago a retired U.S. Steel worker told me that workers steered clear of the "mushroom tops" of hardened steel and slag that remained in crucibles because they sometimes contained the bodies of steelworkers who had fallen in when the material was molten.

In legend, these real-life tragedies become Joe Magarac's triumph, and a suggestion, perhaps, of the steelworker's satisfaction in meeting the test. John Strohmeyer sums up the steelworker's point of view: "It takes uncommon talent, a strong body, and a mind that knows no fear to be able to transform piles of red dirt and scrap into the molten metal that is poured, rolled, and pounded into the various shapes that support the mainframes of civilization." The steelworker has confronted the superhuman in its profoundest, most real sense. Steel is part of him and he is part of it. In Thomas Bell's *Out of This Furnace*, a novel derived from the life of Bell's own family in the mills of Braddock, Mike Dobrejcak, the character modeled on Bell's father, exclaims, despite the wretched working conditions of steel's early days, "Listen to it. When I remember that men built [the mill] it makes me proud I'm a man. If they'd let me I could love that mill like something of my own. It's a terrible and beautiful thing to make iron."

For a hundred years the graves of five of the men who died in the Battle of Homestead remained unmarked in adjoining cemeteries in Homestead. A stone had been placed for John Morris by the Odd Fellows. For the others there had been no money. (The seventh man, George Rutter, had been buried in the town of Verona.) In the summer of 1992, in observance of the Homestead Strike centennial, historians and labor officials placed markers on the graves, and on July 5 held a ceremony to dedicate the markers and honor all seven who died.

I remember walking with the group from grave to grave on that bright July day—present and former steelworkers, men and women of the valley, local and union officials, historians, a Protestant and a Catholic clergyman—to the measured drumbeat of the area's last union band, the National Association of Letter Carriers, Branch 84, AFL-CIO. A stout, gray-haired man in a blue plaid shirt gripped the staff of a gold-fringed American flag that flapped over his head in the wind. Others carried banners: United Steelworkers of America—Pensioners Ass'n.—Homestead District; Amalgamated Association of Iron and Steel Workers of the United States—Homestead Lodges. The new headstones were simple rectangles in the grass, with name and dates engraved above the legend of the fatal day: July 6, 1892. In the upper corners, left and right, were traced the outlines of a cross.

After a hundred years the dead had been given the dignity of a headstone. Peter Ferris, age thirty; Silas Wain, age twenty-five; Thomas Weldon, age thirty; Joseph Sotak, age thirty; Henry Striegel, age nineteen. Sotak and Wain were unskilled laborers who, along with the rest of the unskilled work force, had shown solidarity with the union. Sotak's grave may still be misidentified. In a letter to the *Pittsburgh Post-Gazette*, written in July 1993, the Reverend Dr. Aladar Komjathy cited the following entry from the Book of Registry of Burials of the First Hungarian Reformed Church of Pittsburgh: "Jozsef Szabo, steelworker, Reformed religion, age 33, husband of Erzsebet

Toth, native of Csepely, County of Ung, Hungary, died on July 6, 1892 in Homestead: The cause of death: Bled to death because of the shotwound received during the strike. The burial was conducted in the Homestead Protestant Cemetery on July 8, 1892 by me, Rev. John Kovacs, pastor of the Hungarian Reformed Church of Pittsburgh." Only seven men died. Komjathy suggests that the man we know as Joseph Sotak may actually be Jozsef Szabo, who, in spite of our best intentions, now lies under a stone that bears the wrong name.

In his final remarks the Reverend Alan Morrison, the Methodist clergyman, recalled the mill worker who had asked why we should celebrate these lives now that the mill was closed. "We lose everything," he told him, "if we do not honor those who died for our cause, even if we are met by a new, even greater challenge. The closing of the mill does not negate their courage or their sacrifice."

Above me, at the river's edge, the Fort Duquesne

Bridge looms skyward. The steel of its arch, its

The Contours of Home

slender cables

seem a perfect

blend of authority and grace. Cars move rapidly

along the bridge's upper and lower decks. Light and

shadow play on the sway bracing between the arch

ribs. Over a million pounds of steel reinforce the

bridge's concrete substructure. More than four

miles of steel bearing pile support walls and piers

not founded on rock.

Standing on the bank of the Allegheny near

the Point, looking up at the rise of the arch ribs,

I think of Abram Hewitt's words at the dedication

of the Brooklyn Bridge: "There is not a particle of

matter in it," he said, "which is at rest for the

minutest portion of time." He called the bridge

"instinct with motion." I look hard at the arches of

the Fort Duquesne Bridge and try to imagine the
movement inside.

At the top of the bridge's metal staircase I step
onto the walkway along the bridge's lower deck.
The waters of the Allegheny flow below. The riveted
diagonals of the deck trusses stand to my right. I
run my fingers over the yellow surface of a truss
member. It is slightly rough to the touch. I lay my
hand flat. The pulse of traffic flows through my
palm. I step back. The bridge's shapes of steel seem
stalwart to me, honest, almost alive. I trust their
strength. I know they will keep me safe above the
waters of the river. They have the distant authority
and dependability of a grandfather. I feel taken care
of and am filled with a sense of being at home in
this place.

"Home is land," I read in an essay recently. "Home
is made by generation after generation passing down
fields, homesteads and memories. It is the place
where your mother and father and their mothers

and fathers worked and sweated and married and died." Few of us would think to argue with that statement. The family farm remains a cultural ideal of the engaged, productive life. But as it stands the statement is not full enough. It does not tell the whole story. It leaves out the fact that roots can also be sunk in industrial soil.

I am convinced that the hold Pittsburgh has on me is at least partly genetic, that something in the chemicals I am made of remains ethereally linked to the energy my family invested here. My great-great-grandfather Orin Palmer, a bridge contractor, worked for John and Washington Roebling on their bridge over the Allegheny at Sixth Street, a few blocks upriver from the Point. I know him chiefly by the portrait of his daughter Aurelia, my great-grandmother, that hung in my grandfather's house when I was a child, and from pictures of the bridge, which has since been replaced, in histories of the city. In 1868 the borough of Lawrenceville and a number of townships, including the township of Oakland, were annexed to the city of Pittsburgh. My great-great-uncle William Kennedy, a gentle bachelor and locating engineer for railroads, was appointed district engineer in charge of determining new thoroughfares and connecting the streets of the villages with those of the city. In 1871 he became chief engineer of the Pittsburgh New Water-Works, siting and overseeing the construction of reservoirs and piping systems still used by the city today. One of those reservoirs sits on the portion of hill that rises above the copper green domes of Immaculate Heart of Mary Church, set on midslope further up the Allegheny.

On the near bank of the Ohio below the Point is the site of the rolling mill in which my great-grandfather Albert Graham worked when he was young. He would eventually become owner of the Graham Nut Company, with offices on the same stretch of riverbank. The company's plant building still stands on Neville Island. Over the entrance portal of the building's brick front, a concrete medallion carries a monogram G, set against the vertical axis of a bolt. The letter nestles between the head of the bolt above and the nut at the bottom which forms a base.

Near the rolling mill site where my great-grandfather worked is a railroad trestle that once belonged to the Pittsburgh & West Virginia Railway. The railroad's former yards are several miles behind the bluff that lines the river. My grandfather, Charles Graham, was president of the railroad when I was young, and it is he of all these forebears whom I actually knew, a flamboyant, generous man, deemed not quite socially acceptable by Pittsburgh's elite, who left school at fourteen and worked for the family nut company, then for its corporate successor, Pittsburgh Screw & Bolt. As president of the railroad he often took us on excursions on the *Westmoreland,* the private car he had on loan from the daughter of Henry Clay Frick. (She allowed him to use it on condition that he scrap it when he was through with it—she didn't want it turned into a diner.) I remember playing in the yards as we waited to board, playing tightrope walker on the tracks, amid the clatter of cars being moved, the attenuated squeal of brakes, the thump of metal couplings being joined. Across the road from the yards, in Chartiers Cemetery, is the grave of John Graham, my great-great-grandfather, born in 1806, a blacksmith.

What impresses me is that when I came back to Pittsburgh I chose an apartment, without being aware of it, virtually at the center of my family's history. It is only since I have returned that I have assigned actual locations to what for me were abstract facts about my family or memories geographically unfixed. Much of my family history is represented in landmarks I can see from my window. It is surely more than fancy to believe that my family has brought me home.

When I look out over the city I see my family, all families, making their home, adapting the natural world to their needs. Just as any other animal does. I ask myself if I would feel so drawn to this place if a pall of smoke still hung over it. It's a fair question. And one I can't answer. But it doesn't seem to have bothered my family. One of my cousins said to me recently, "We just had two sets of curtains and one was always in the wash." (I should admit she wasn't the one who did the wash.) A retired steelworker reminded me that "with the rusty belch of an open hearth came a check." Writer David McCullough, who grew up in Pittsburgh, has said, "To me it's always been a beautiful city, even in the supposedly 'bad old days.'"

Pittsburgh is a city of neighborhoods: Polish Hill, Bloomfield, South Side slopes, South Side flats, Oakland, Morningside, Homewood—ninety in all. Today, their names appear on street signs above the name of the street. It is often said that people here identify themselves first by their neighborhood and only then as part of the larger entity, the city. Several years ago, the general manager of Prime Sports, which owned the cable rights to the Pirates, made some deeply insulting remarks about Lanny Frattare, the team's play-by-play announcer for over twenty years. When I wrote in Frattare's defense to the editor of the *Pittsburgh Post-Gazette*, I received a postcard by return mail asking to know my neighborhood. I told them that I live in Mt. Washington, an area on the ridge of the same name.

Each neighborhood is unique. Some are particularly characteristic. The narrow, gable-roofed houses of working people climb the South Side slopes of the Monongahela densely, in jumbled rows, above the turn-of-the-century commercial buildings and row houses of the South Side flats and the expanse of empty land that was once part of the Pittsburgh Works of Jones & Laughlin Steel. Perched on the hillside, they call to mind an Italian hill town, holding perpendicular against the plunging angle of the hill. With the mills closed down, their faces glow white in the sunlight above the red brick of the flats.

In neighborhoods more removed from the rivers, long lines of solid brick houses with sturdy brick porches look out on precipitously sloping front lawns. The slope is accented, house after house, by concrete steps leading from porch to sidewalk. Produce wholesalers and ethnic markets, machine shops and small foundries, and now nightclubs thrive in the Strip District along the downtown side of the Allegheny. The three-hundred-acre strip of land was home to the founding plants of Westinghouse Air Brake and Alcoa, as well as to the city's earliest iron foundries. In one of history's curious turns, the Westinghouse building now houses RedZone Robotics, which specializes in robots designed to investigate and clean up hazardous waste.

Oakland is monumental Pittsburgh, where the Cathedral of Learning, the forty-story, Gothic-inspired classroom building at the University of Pittsburgh, stands like a beacon in a wide, green lawn. Across the avenue is the huge, Beaux-Arts Carnegie Library, the library's main branch, and Carnegie Institute, with museums of art and natural history, a music hall and a lecture hall. The site is flanked by the eclectic quadrangle of Carnegie Mellon University (the university is renowned as a center for computer science, robotics, and artificial intelligence), and by Schenley Park, whose vistas and serpentine drives were shaped by landscape architect William Falconer.

However individual, the neighborhoods are visually unified by the necessity of accommodating to the terrain (fully one-third of the city is green with vegetation, largely because of slopes too steep to build on) and by the prevalence of churches. Throughout the city, steeples, towers, and onion domes rise from clusters of gabled rooftops, nestle against the walls of skyscrapers, or stand out against the horizon at the tops of hills. My favorite example is a classic Pittsburgh vista I pass often at the base of Mt. Washington—the eight domes and golden three-bar crosses of the Byzantine Rite Saint John the Baptist Ukrainian Catholic Church lifting against a backdrop of skyscrapers across the river, lending an air of exotic mystery to a modern scene.

Many neighborhoods have been intimate with industry. Railroad tracks and trestles curve through clusters of houses, over backyards and neighborhood streets, even carve an elevated arc through the upper edge of downtown. Particularly in central neighborhoods and along the rivers, houses mingle with warehouses and small workshops or older industrial buildings made of brick. Until recently, blast furnaces stood at the side of one of the major roadways into the city.

A visiting friend remarked to me, "There's so much visually going on here." Pediments and cornice brackets, trusses, gables, steeples, domes, long metal roofs, ductwork and stacks, the city's compactness gives it a sort of visual syncopation as the scene changes from street to street, neighborhood to neighborhood, layer outlined against layer like a series of stage sets growing out of the rising, retreating hills.

For much of its history, Pittsburgh was a city not just of neighborhoods but of ethnic neighborhoods. Though ethnic populations have tended to disperse since World War II, large populations of Italians still live in Bloomfield, as do Germans in Troy Hill, Spring Hill, and Dutchtown, Jews in Squirrel Hill, and Polish in Polish Hill. The city's ethnic neighborhoods have been a major source of its stability and its sense of community. When I began work on this book, I realized I needed to experience that sort of neighborhood firsthand, to get a sense of what it has meant to live, generation after generation, in a small, close-knit parcel of the city. I decided to explore Polish Hill. The neighborhood has changed over time and is no longer almost uniformly Polish. But the core values that gave immigrant communities their strength are still represented there. As it turned out, my time in Polish Hill would give me a keen sense of what was positive in the immigrant experience. It would also show me how a community may forge bonds to an industrial landscape.

In the quiet of a sunny July morning, the domes of Immaculate Heart of Mary Church reign serenely over the rooftops of Polish Hill. Since its consecration in 1905 on its precarious hillside site, the church has been the center of life in the neighborhood. The majestic basilica of brick and limestone was built largely by the parishioners themselves, many of them workers in the mills of the Strip District below. The document listing the contributors and builders of the church is sealed in a locket on the statue of the Virgin on the main altar. For a neighborhood church it seems huge—200 feet in length and 110 feet wide. Its central dome rises 138 feet and is topped by a 12-foot cross. Its seating capacity is eighteen hundred people.

Beneath the domes, rows of houses, three or four stories tall, with narrow fronts largely free of ornament, cluster on the hillside like matchboxes standing on end. Streets fork off, come together at angles, and backyards merge like shapes in a kaleidoscope. As I climb the steep slope of Brereton Avenue toward the church, I note the brick or frame of the house fronts, the grass pushing through the herringbone brick sidewalk, the rows of zinnias, petunias, tiger lilies, and tomato plants glimpsed through passageways between the tall building walls. At more than one house, vines are heavy with unripened grapes. I can smell pastries baking.

Not far from the church a roofing contractor scrapes shingles from the steep pitch of a roof. Up the avenue city workers break up a curb with jackhammers. A woman sits with two young children on a stoop. Once part of the neighborhood's chief commercial area, the street is largely empty of shops. In the angle formed as Dobson Street forks off from Brereton is a memorial honoring those of the neighborhood who have served in war.

During the years of mass immigration from eastern and southern Europe, tens of thousands of hitherto rural people carved a home for themselves in the unfamiliar urban landscape of Pittsburgh. They were strangers in a new country, ridiculed by the predominantly northern European population that had preceded them for their peasant traditions, their unintelligible speech, and their willingness to work hard at the meanest occupations. Largely on their own they built communities that would sustain them, in which the values they had lived by could take root. Italians, Poles, Slovaks, Croatians, Ukrainians, Carpatho-Rusyns, among others formed national churches in which services could be conducted in their own language and according to their own liturgy. Saint Stanislaus Kostka, the mother church of the Polish community, began in 1875 in the Strip District as a small chapel with a school in the basement. By 1892 the community had built the present-day Saint Stanislaus Kostka, eventually known more familiarly as Saint Stan's, and had acquired an adjacent building which housed a school serving seven hundred students. Only blocks away stood Saint Elizabeth of Hungary, the mother church of the Slovak community, which was dedicated in 1895. Members of one ethnic group were often reluctant to attend services in a church of different ethnic makeup. Italian Catholics in Bloomfield gathered in a former blacksmith shop, rather than at the local German Catholic church, before building their own church in 1905.

Ethnic churches and fraternal and beneficial organizations played a major role in the community's secular life as social centers, as organisms for charitable fundraising and insurance, as sources of credit (the city's banks were unwilling as a rule to lend money to this new wave of immigrants), and as preservers of old-country culture. Lodges of such organizations as the Polish Falcons served as meeting places and as sponsors of athletic, musical, and social events. Organizations like the Greek Catholic Union, the National Slavonic Society, the First Catholic Slovak Union, and the National Croatian Society paid death and disability benefits. In 1908, according to Pittsburgh Survey author Margaret Byington, the Greek Catholic Union paid $400 for the death of a husband or a wife, $1,000 for total disability, $300 for the loss of a limb, and $150 for the loss of an eye, events that were all too common in industrial life.

Poles began settling on this previously undeveloped 139-acre site around 1885, traveling on foot between their homes on the hillside and their work in the mills below. After little more than a decade the neighborhood had grown substantially, and the trek between Saint Stanislaus Kostka and home had proved to be too dangerous. Churchgoers and children attending school had to cross the Pennsylvania Railroad tracks and two sets of trolley tracks to reach their destination. In 1895 the residents of Polish Hill requested permission of the Pittsburgh diocese to establish a parish and to build their own church and school. They named their parish Immaculate Heart of Mary.

The building that once housed Immaculate Heart of Mary School stands behind the church on Paulowna Street. It is a burly building of soot-covered red brick, with Romanesque arches over the windows and a rust-red-painted fire escape leading from roof to sidewalk. The arches over the windows are echoed in the repeated pairs of conjoined verticals in the metal fence bordering the small park alongside. Completed in 1897, the building contained ten rooms for school use and also served as the living quarters of the teaching nuns. The upper floor was used as a temporary church. At the time, there were 493 families in the parish.

Harry Harenski, a retired machinist who celebrated his one-hundredth birthday in July 1996, recalls playing in the brick yard on the site where Immaculate Heart of Mary Church now stands. A balding, voluble man, slender and slightly stooped, he lives alone on Bethoven Street after the death of his wife five years ago. I have heard that he has just had his driver's license renewed, although he no longer drives at night. As he welcomes me into his neatly appointed living room, he gestures toward the leather chair that Peter Falk sat in during the filming of *Roommates,* based on a story by Max Apple and filmed partly in Polish Hill. When told by the film's advance people that Falk would be coming, Harry responded, referring to the Columbo character for which Falk is best known, "Tell him to ditch the raincoat. And don't park that jalopy in front of my house." Perched on the television set is a white baseball cap sporting the number 100, given to him in honor of his birthday by the tellers at the bank.

Harry's father had a grocery across from the church site. He had come to this country from Poland with his mother and four siblings and had, as Harry phrased it, "drifted into the steel mills and lived in the Strip." Harry's mother was born in Pittsburgh's South Side and it was she who would teach her Polish-born husband how to read and write. Harry was the first of his family to be baptized "on the Hill," on the top floor of the school, instead of at Saint Stan's. One of a family of ten, he completed Immaculate Heart of Mary School, but was unable to go on to high school. The closest high school at the time was Central downtown, and the nickel trolley fare each way was more than his father could afford. "Kids would go through sixth or eighth grade," Harry said, "and then go out and get a job to help the family. Boys would go to Kress Box Company on Twenty-eighth Street, or to Pittsburgh Screw & Bolt on Twenty-fourth. Girls would go to the cigar factories in the Strip, the cork or wool factories, or candy factories. At one time you'd see a crowd of twenty or thirty girls walking up from the Strip, and you could smell the tobacco on them."

Harry got "shot up" in the war in France four to five weeks before the armistice and came back to this country on a stretcher. He holds out his legs to demonstrate that one is shorter than the other. Army doctors had to graft a piece of bone from his lower leg to repair his femur. He was in a cast for six to eight months. When he healed, he started work in the machine shop of a plant on the South Side that manufactured railroad spikes and fishplates. He had no skills, he said. "I was a green Polish Hunky kid. What the hell did I know?"

I ask Harry to tell me about playing as a boy on the work site during the building of Immaculate Heart of Mary Church. His face shows the beginning of a smile. Blocks of limestone, he says, were hauled by horse and wagon from the railroad below to be shaped on the street by masons using wooden hammers and chisels.

"What was a kid going to do?" he asked. "The masons left their chisels out at night. How could a kid resist?" Two of the chisels found their way into Harry's possession. "I was scared to death my dad would find out," Harry said. "He would have killed me. So I hid them in the stable."

I ask Harry to tell me what people did for fun. "This was the noisiest place in Pittsburgh," Harry declared of Polish Hill in the 1930s. "There used to be fifteen to eighteen christenings a month." For the celebration afterward, parents would order in a bottle of whiskey and a case of beer from one of the wholesale houses, to go with ham and bread, sweet bread and kielbasa. A young men's concertina combo would provide the music. "There were fifteen hundred kids running around," Harry said. "Every Sunday."

People made their own entertainment, Harry said. The dances on Friday or Saturday night were packed. Any excuse was used for a parade. The nearby West Penn playground featured two to three baseball games a week. The semipro Immaculate Heart of Mary team belonged to the City League, and the Negro League's Pittsburgh Crawfords and Homestead Grays both played games in the neighborhood. "Satchel Paige and all those guys used to come down here," Harry said. "We thought nothing of it."

Houses in Polish Hill had few conveniences. All had outhouses at the back when they were built, either on the porch or in the yard. Coal stoves provided heat. Helen Wolkiewicz, another longtime resident of Polish Hill, remembers her father, a machinist at Crucible Steel, "coming home from the mill black." As the house had no bathroom, he rigged up a shower in the basement out of a sprinkling can hanging on a wire. Vicki Pleczkowski recalls her father heating water in a galvanized tub. All seven children would line up for a bath, using the same water, one by one. Helen W. remembers that after her mother did the laundry, boiling the whites, her father would take the wash water to flush the outhouses. Many houses were built by the owners themselves. Punchy Zielmanski tells of taking the roof off his father-in-law's house and being amazed at the hodgepodge he found—not evenly spaced rafters but all sorts of pieces of differing size, whatever they could get hold of. "Still, it was good wood," he said. "Not what you see nowadays."

Today, of course, the houses have been modernized. On the day I went to call on Sharon Wolkiewicz and her mother Helen, Sharon met me near the church and we walked together down the slope. Sharon is a handsome, gentle woman, with short blond hair, probably in her forties. Nearing her house, the last before the end of the street, we looked out over the rooftops of plant sheds in the Strip District below. They were surprisingly light in color, a pattern of clean-looking lines. I had the sense that if I leaned out over the street barrier I would be able to reach down and almost touch them. Beyond the rooftops was the broad sweep of hills rising from the far bank of the Allegheny.

Sharon's living room is on the first floor, a light, airy room with filmy white curtains. The kitchen behind it has been lately remodeled, with attractive, pale wood cabinets. In the bedroom, to the right as we walked from living room to kitchen, a white cat with touches of tortoiseshell lay on the chenille bedspread pretending to sleep, its head curled upside down, checking us out through one slitted eye. On the second floor, Sharon's mother's rooms are more humble. The kitchen, which we entered at the top of the stairs, is of earlier vintage, with black-

and-white linoleum tiles. Helen greeted us from the living room, leaning on her walker, a small, jolly woman with red hair. She gestured me to a couch in the corner by the window and then sat down across from me in her overstuffed chair, a sort of nest with magazines, telephone, and television within easy reach. Sharon pulled over a straight chair and sat facing her mother. Helen mentioned that she was looking forward to her polka program on PBS at four-thirty.

I asked Helen to tell me about her memories of Polish Hill. She thought for a moment, then replied. "It was a very happy life," she said. "We didn't have nothin'." It is interesting to note that in my conversations with people in Polish Hill, I encountered none of the outrage expressed by reformers like Margaret Byington. Again and again, it was the happiness residents chose to remember in what had to be often difficult lives. I remember asking a group of women at the senior center if they had resented the dirt from the mills. They replied in a chorus, "Yes!" But that isn't what they wanted to tell me about, giving way possibly to what sociologist Corinne Azen Krause calls the "human tendency to hide the unpleasant." Still, whatever their motives, there is no denying that these are people who, for the most part, simply went about doing what needed to be done.

Helen was born on the hill and has lived in this house since her father bought it when she was seven, in 1924. "It was a gold mine," she exclaimed, in an attempt to convey the enormity of her father's investment. Both parents had come directly to Pittsburgh from Poland. Her mother had come on her own, doing live-in housework before marrying at Immaculate Heart of Mary in 1915. Because the language of the household was Polish, Helen learned English at school and from English-speaking children on the street.

Helen attended all eight grades at Immaculate Heart of Mary School, where she was taught Polish history and language, Bible, catechism, and prayers, in addition to standard subjects. Every morning at seven-thirty the students gathered in the schoolyard to go to mass. After completing Immaculate Heart of Mary she went on to Bellefield Trade School to study sewing. She was expected to do chores at home, cleaning the outdoor toilets and, every Friday, scrubbing the downstairs hallway on her knees. When she was older she did the dishes. Sometimes, she told me with a grin, when she was supposed to go to a dance at the Polish club on the hill, she would hide dishes in the stove while her mother was out of the room instead of taking the time to wash them. She would return from the dance to meet her mother "and the heel of a shoe."

"Polish people are happy people," Helen says. She remembers those dances at the Polish club, which featured big name bands for an admission charge of twenty-five cents. Near the church on Brereton Avenue, Pittsburgh's first Polish Lyceum offered pool tables and a bowling alley. Helen and her friends would chip in a total of $1.25 every Sunday to go bowling. Week-long street fairs were held on the site, with game booths, bands, a Polish kitchen, and yellow lights strung across the yard. In the Lyceum auditorium plays were put on by the Filaret Society, formed by Father Michael Sonnefeld to "spread truth and virtue and to bring culture to the poor class of society."

Sharon is Helen's daughter by her second husband. Helen's first husband, an Italian by the name of Paiano, worked for Sunshine Biscuit on Thirty-fourth Street. He died of tuberculosis twelve years after they were married. Helen worked at Liberty Cleaners in Bloomfield and then as head dishwasher at Schenley High School until Sharon was born. Sharon's father worked for a welding company and tended bar on the side. The family lived on the second floor of the house, where Helen still lives; Helen's parents lived on the first floor. At various times, an aunt and uncle or a cousin lived on the third floor.

Helen says she is "embedded here." Both her husbands came to live in her parents' house. She has loved Polish Hill since she was a little kid, she says, and still has close friends here. When I ask her to tell me more about her early life, she recalls the children of the neighborhood going around together, playing games, chasing tin cans, baking potatoes in a fire outside until they were burnt black, then eating them plain. "My brother called them 'potooties'!" she exclaimed, then laughed.

Sharon has comparable memories. An office clerk and assistant manager in a ninety-year-old company in Oakland, she points to the unity of people in Polish Hill, the values they have lived by. "I could never leave here," she says. She remembers the church playing Christmas carols outside on a loudspeaker, decorating her grandmother's Christmas tree with ornaments stored in "a valise." From time to time a photographer came to the neighborhood to take pictures of the children on his pony. "How could you just move away," she asks, "and call another place home?" I press Sharon on this point, and she adds, "I've never wanted to go anywhere else. It's the family heritage, but it's also something deeper. It gets into your blood. This is where I belong."

In many ways the neighborhood is not what it was. With the exodus of families to the suburbs after World War II and the closing of nearby mills in the 1970s, few stores remain, and the population is down dramatically from its high point in the early 1940s. "This was a dynamite neighborhood," Richard "Punchy" Zielmanski told me. "The streets were jammed with people. There were shoe stores, fruit stores, bakeries, butchers, drugstores, furniture stores, taverns, barbers, hardware stores, doctors, dentists, florists. You never had to leave the hill. Now people shop in the Strip or in Bloomfield. I watched it all evaporate. We're just trying to hold the hill together now. I never thought it would be that way."

I sat with Punchy one afternoon on a bench next to the war memorial. At fifty-nine, he has lived all his life in Polish Hill. He remembers his father working "like the devil" sixteen hours a day during the war at the Pennsylvania Railroad produce yards in the Strip District and at nearby Crucible Steel. When he died at the age of forty-six, of Hodgkin's disease, the family found rooms in the back, two upstairs and two down, in the house of Toni Dobies's grandmother. (I would meet Toni Dobies later.) He points at a street that angles off behind us, the eighth house down. Punchy's mother went out to work after her husband died, as a nighttime cleaning woman. Her husband hadn't wanted her to work when he was alive.

"She loved to dance," Punchy recalled. "After he died, she went to dances on Friday or Saturday nights at the vets' club in Lawrenceville, the Falcons, the Polish Eagles. She couldn't do it before. He wasn't much of a dancer." Punchy remembers his mother taking him to Goodwill to buy him a pair of shoes. She couldn't afford much. He is still moved by the intensity of her effort to provide for him.

Punchy works on an assembly line in the vinegar department at Heinz. When they hired him they told him there would be a two-month probation period. "I'm not scared of work," he told them. "I'll tackle any job, it don't bother me." He says assembly line work is not boring. The line has to be rolling. The day flies by. You don't have to be strong, he says, but you have to be fast. I remind him of the *I Love Lucy* segment in which Lucy is hired to box candies passing on a conveyer.

"That's it!" he exclaims. He likes the people he works with, the process.

When asked about the old days in Polish Hill, he mentions "the hordes of kids" in the streets. "Everyone in the neighborhood watched out for each other," he says. "If your mother couldn't breast-feed, someone else would!" He remembers sneaking up to his grandmother's house to eat. He loved her homemade soups—vegetable, duck (made with duck's blood), beet—and her pork chops, city chicken, sauerkraut, and ham. "When they cooked, they threw in a handful of everything and you et!" he exclaimed. He is appalled at the waste he sees around him. "In those days," he said, "if you didn't eat it, your brother would. The plates were shiny when we finished."

Punchy sees himself as a sort of neighborhood watchdog. He has painted the benches at the war memorial repeatedly to hide graffiti. He is also on the church council and has gotten himself on the Democratic Committee, not for glory, he says, but to try to help the community get things done. Last year he helped to organize Minor, Little League, and Pony League teams in the neighborhood. He pulls out snapshots of one of the teams at a recent game in their uniform black shirts and white pants. In the same packet of pictures is one of his younger daughter, who still lives at home, performing on the South Side as part of an ethnic dance group sponsored by the Polish Alliance. Punchy's older daughter lives on the corner behind where we are sitting. His son works for the city and lives on Paulowna Street.

Punchy's wife Millie is a pretty woman, a little plump, with short dark hair. She was born across the street from where we sit, in her grandparents' house, now a vacant lot. Millie stops to say something to Punchy, and the subject turns to Father Joe Swierczynski, the new pastor of Immaculate Heart of Mary

Church. Father Joe has recently taken over at the church and has restored a number of traditional forms of observance that had been allowed to lapse there.

Punchy recalls Father Joe washing his feet on Holy Thursday as, dressed in a white robe, he appeared as one of the twelve apostles. On Good Friday he was among those who carried the statue of Jesus. The men carried the statue around the inside of the church, crossing twice in front of the altar, then placed it in a makeshift tomb to one side. The organ thundered; the lights, like lightning, flashed and then went out. The verisimilitude was almost overwhelming. "I felt like I would start to cry," Millie says. "I said to my daughter, 'It's like this is really happening!'"

Father Joe Swierczynski is a personable, informal man, down-to-earth like his parishioners, a short man with dense, wavy dark blond hair. He has furnished his office in the rectory with a graceful French Provincial-style desk, an oriental rug, and wing chairs that echo the curves of the desk's cabriole legs. A showcase behind the desk displays his personal collection of biblical and church-related figurines. Father Joe was born in Sharpsburg of American parents; his grandparents had come to this country in the late 1890s. Both grandfathers worked in the steel mills, his maternal grandfather at Spang's in Sharpsburg. He clearly cherishes the ethnic traditions he grew up with and is intent on restoring them at Immaculate Heart of Mary. Observing the traditions reinforces his parishioners' ethnic identity, he says. It gives them a sense of pride in their culture and brings them closer to God. At times in his life when he was located in a place where the traditions weren't being observed, Father Joe says, "I was dying."

I ask Father Joe about the *Wilia* meal on Christmas Eve that Helen and Sharon had mentioned to me. The family all comes together, he says, wherever they live. Before the dinner, the youngest in the family looks for a star. When he sees one the dinner may start. If it's cloudy the family waits until it would be dark enough to see a star if the sky were clear. Straw is put under the tablecloth to symbolize Christ, and an extra place setting, using the family's best china and silverware, is placed either at the end of the table or at the center, wherever it is most visible, to keep the diners aware that the celebration is for Christ. Some families put straw under the table. Traditional foods are served—mushroom soup, pierogi, different kinds of fish, fruit compote, noodles with poppy seeds, sauerkraut with peas, for example, but no meat.

After the meal comes the sharing of the *Oplatek,* a large, rectangular, unleavened wafer like the host received at mass. The wafer, which bears a Nativity scene, a scene of the three kings, or some other comparable image, has been broken into pieces and is placed at the center of the table. After the meal, each person takes a piece of wafer and offers it to another; the other person breaks off a piece and offers the first person good wishes. One might wish a child good luck in school, a pregnant woman good wishes for the baby. Then the person who has received the good wishes breaks off a piece of the other's wafer and reciprocates, and the exchange is repeated until each person has greeted everyone in the room. As I listen to Father Joe, I begin to think of the concentration of goodwill, the eye-to-eye focus of individual on individual that takes place with the sharing of the *Oplatek.* I begin to imagine how the ceremonial recognition of each person must strengthen individual and family bonds. I also begin to wonder at what we may be losing when, as in Protestant churches, we abandon many concrete symbols of faith. A friend of mine recently remarked to me that she loves the spirituality of her church (if not the legality). As I listened to Father Joe, I began to appreciate how spirituality becomes manifest in tangible things.

Throughout the first part of our conversation, Father Joe has been summoned out of his office repeatedly to answer questions or to advise in the preparations for a funeral service that is to take place later in the morning. He apologizes again as he returns and sits in the wing chair a few feet from mine.

"Easter is the biggest holiday for the Polish church," he says. He loves putting it all together, the pageantry of Holy Thursday and Good Friday, Saturday's Easter Vigil Mass and Sunday's Easter Mass in celebration of the risen Christ. Father Joe has also reinstated the typically Polish Resurrection procession around the outside of the church which precedes the Easter morning Mass. In the procession of apostles, servers, and children are carried a crucifix with a red stole symbolizing Christ's victory over death; a statue of the risen Christ; the paschal candle symbolizing the light of Christ; and, carried by the priest, a monstrance containing the Sacrament. Blessed on Holy Saturday, the paschal candle is used throughout the year at every funeral and baptism as a symbol of continuity, of linking life's landmarks to the light of Christ.

On Easter Saturday parishioners bring baskets containing the food to be served at the first meal of Easter morning to the church to be blessed: bread, butter, ham, cakes, eggs. "The church aisle is full of kielbasa and such," Father Joe says. "The blessing has to be offered three or four times that day to cover everyone. The church couldn't contain it all at one time." He remembers as a child "Hunkies" being laughed at for getting their food blessed. "It used to be just us and the Slovaks," he said. "Now everybody is doing it."

Certain elements of the meal have symbolic value. The egg represents the Resurrection, horseradish the bitter herbs at the Last Supper, wine the bitter wine given to Christ on the cross. "God blesses the food," Father Joe says, "and the people are grateful for what they have, which God has given them." Slices of egg are exchanged at Easter as pieces of wafer are exchanged at Christmas. Before Christmas and Easter houses are cleaned "from head to toe." Everything is scrubbed down and children are assigned their own special tasks. "It's a big time for them," Father Joe says. "This way they know that it's not just Santa Claus and the Easter Bunny."

In all of this I am particularly struck by, in fact perhaps for the first time begin to understand, the profound linkage that can exist between religious and domestic life, the interplay between church and home, how even now, at the end of the twentieth century, religious faith can imbue people's secular lives and how age-old traditions can unify a community and bind it to a place. There seems to be such a sense here of what is important. "The people of Polish Hill are happy with what they have," Father Joe says. "They're not trying to live beyond their means." As I write this, I even feel a bit uneasy, as if it may not be credible to a reader. We are so removed as a culture from this sort of balance. And yet, the picture painted here, of this small group of people, is well grounded. "There is too much money, money, money," Sharon Wolkiewicz said to me. "Many people in Polish Hill realize that and want to live according to truer values."

They are aware of the challenge their neighborhood faces. Overall, the neighborhood has gotten older; many residents live as couples or alone in houses that once numbered a family to each floor. Although the church is self-sustaining, the school came to represent a significant drain on parish resources. Parishioners held frequent fundraising events—bake sales and the like—along with the parish festival and various raffles. But their efforts came up short. In June 1997, it was announced that Immaculate Heart of Mary School would close.

There are positive trends. Some families who had moved to the suburbs, or their children, are coming back, because it is less expensive and because they miss the traditions they knew. After months of undercover work, police succeeded in breaking up a drug ring that had been operating on Herron Avenue. The houses which served as its headquarters have since been condemned and torn down, and new housing is going up on the site.

Toni Dobies feels that the reason for the neighborhood's success is that it lives "in God's shadow," in the aura cast by the church's towering green domes. "It is why we are so blessed," she says. "Our traditions make us rich, not financially, but in terms of a blessed life." Toni's children are fourth-generation Polish Hill on her side, fifth generation on her husband Mark's. Both of Toni's grandfathers worked in steel mills, her paternal grandfather at Jones & Laughlin, where he worked his way up to foreman, and her maternal grandfather at Carnegie Steel, which fired him, she says, only days before he qualified for his pension. He was hired by the Pennsylvania Railroad and worked until he was close to eighty. Toni's father worked at Heppenstall Forge in Lawrenceville. Her husband Mark is an operations manager at the city's asphalt plant. Toni resents the fact that management did not appreciate the steelworker's skill. Her father could look at molten steel, she said, and know it wouldn't be a good batch. The managers didn't understand the degree of skill that could be achieved through experience by formally uneducated people.

Toni is an energetic woman with dark, wavy hair and clear, gray-blue eyes. This morning she is wearing a blouse with a splashy jungle print. She has just finished her baking and small, fruit-filled pastries called *kolaczki* are cooling on racks on the counter by the stove. She speaks with assurance, and after only a few minutes of conversation it is obvious that she is a woman who knows what she thinks and who knows how to get things done.

"Children in Polish Hill are taught that what is most important in life is God, family, community," Toni says, "in that order." Toni herself is part of a program to discourage membership in gangs, meeting with kids at a neutral site in city neighborhoods most at risk. "Kids are preying on each other in some neighborhoods," she says. She describes turning over a gallon jug of water to show the children how quickly we bleed to death.

As a child Toni was impatient with religious rituals, but now finds herself requiring of her children what her mother required of her. The family tries to say the rosary every evening at seven o'clock, just as her mother did. She has noticed lately that her prayers for others seem to have an uncanny tendency to come true. She stops for a moment and looks me in the eye, to be sure, I think, that I am not taking her statement lightly. She is convinced that God is working through her. I sense that she is gratified to have her mother's faith confirmed by her own experience.

For over a century Polish Hill residents have stuck together. "The common ideal of the neighborhood is the sense of community," says Chris Potochnik of the Polish Hill Civic Association, "the sense of loyalty to one another. These are people who had a rough time. Everyone had to stick together to make the neighborhood work and provide for their families. That's how they survived." Sharon Wolkiewicz carried the thought further. "I think the hard times made them happier," she said.

"They knew they were struggling to achieve what they believed in, and the shared struggle made them stronger."

One sees a darker view of industrial life in Saint Nicholas Croatian Catholic Church in Millvale. Rising on the side of a hill overlooking the Allegheny valley floor, the church has a somewhat unprepossessing exterior, its walls of undistinguished yellow brick bearing little suggestion of the treasures inside. It was the second church to be built by Pittsburgh's Croatian community, the first being Saint Nicholas Northside a few miles downriver. After a devastating fire in 1921, and subsequent reconstruction, the Croatian painter Maximilian (Maxo) Vanka was commissioned to paint the church's interior walls. Executed in two sessions in 1937 and 1941, Vanka's murals are an extraordinary integration of the secular and the holy and a powerful indictment of evil.

On entering this small, working-class church, one is struck first by its snugness, its intimacy, the gleam of its graceful, richly varnished pews. There is a sense that the church is cherished, and that it cherishes in turn, with a spiritual embrace echoed in the curves of the ceiling's cross and barrel vaults. Rich reds, blues, greens, and browns cover ceilings and walls, presided over by the startling figure of the Virgin in the apse above the altar. On the arch over the altar is an inscription that reads "Marijo-Kraljice Hrvata-moli za nas" (Mary, queen of Croatians, pray for us).

Vanka's bold Byzantine-postured Madonna, seated on her throne, looks out at the viewer with sad, hooded eyes. Her sturdy hands hold her child, who stands, facing the viewer, on her solid left thigh. Unlike a true Byzantine Madonna, this crowned Madonna, in red dress and flowing blue cape, holding her similarly crowned child, is a peasant, a robust woman of the people who knows physical work. Folk motifs adorn her dress and her throne. Other folk motifs appear on the building's vault ribs.

Vanka's identification with the people makes his murals for the church an anguished protest. To one side of the altar, below the Virgin and Child, peasants in native dress pray in pastoral Croatia; to the other side, industrial workers offer their church to the Holy Mother as smoke billows from the stacks of the Allegheny valley mills. Below the workers is an image of the bearded Vanka, added in the 1970s, with a child seated on his lap, a bird on his right foot. Legend has it that a sparrow, which Vanka had nursed back to health after it had broken its wing, sat on his shoulder as he worked.

Throughout the church, murals reminiscent of Orozco and Rivera portray, with an interweaving of traditional religious iconography, the ravages of industrialism and war, and the recurrent image of mothers shedding tears over the death of sons. On the front wall of one of the short transepts the Blessed Mother weeps at the Crucifixion; on the front wall of the other the Mother of Sorrows weeps in a Pietà.

On the rear transept wall, opposite the Pietà, peasant women in identical flowing white dresses grieve in community over the casket of a young soldier in rural Croatia, as a field of white crosses carries the viewer's eye up the hill to a small, white church. On the wall opposite the Crucifixion, women in dark dress echoing that of the Virgin of the transept murals grieve over the body of a young man killed in a mining accident in Johnstown, as more men descend toward the mine with pickaxes over their shoulders. The corpse lies on a sheet of newspaper which reports in Croatian: "American mothers raise their sons to be victims of American industry."

Other companion paintings expand on these themes. On the wall under the choir a top-hatted capitalist dines sumptuously, alone, served by a black butler, ignoring the outstretched palm of a beggar. His face is a face of death. On the opposite wall a humble Croatian family shares a simple meal imbued with the spirit of Christ who stands behind them against the background of the Allegheny valley.

On one of the side walls, the figure of divine justice is opposed by the grotesque figure of injustice, who wears a gas mask and, in one hand, carries a bloody sword. In her other hand she holds the scales of justice in which bread is outweighed by gold. On the ceiling under the choir the Virgin, her eyes wide with horror, separates two World War I soldiers, pushing away the bayoneted barrel of a gun. In the painting next to it, a soldier's bayonet punctures the graphically depicted heart of a stricken Christ.

Diane Novosel is head of the Society for the Preservation of the Murals of Saint Nicholas Millvale. The granddaughter of Croatian and Romanian immigrants, she is a tall, dark-haired woman in her forties with a rich, almost operatic voice and an equally big heart, whose family story is a paradigm of the American ethnic experience. She told me her story as we sat together on a park bench one cool July evening. She was still keyed up after a long day as a clinical social worker at a nearby hospital, and her memories spilled out easily, with the authority of someone who has given her life a good deal of thought.

Diane's paternal grandfather worked at a variety of mills and forges before securing a position at Pittsburgh Rolls, where he remained until his death. He had been born in the mountains in Croatia and had come to the U.S. as a young man, sponsored by a cousin and starting life in a boarding house in Lawrenceville. It was at the boarding house that he met the young Croatian immigrant woman who would become his first wife. While working twelve hours a day, he attended classes to learn English and often acted as an interpreter in the neighborhood or as a translator of legal documents and correspondence. He also sponsored a brother-in-law and a sister-in-law who came to the U.S. and settled in the same Pittsburgh community.

When his wife died seven months after giving birth to their fourth child, his wife's sister came from Croatia to care for the children. They eventually married and had three more children, one of whom was Diane's father. Even during the Depression, Diane's grandfather, by then a foreman, had work at the mill, although his hours and wages were unpredictable, and his wife supplemented the family income by doing sewing at home. The oldest children left high school to find jobs and contribute to the family. After their father died at the age of sixty-one, it was up to all six older siblings, who by then were self-sufficient, to care for their mother, their grandmother (who had followed her daughter to America), and their teenaged sister.

Diane's mother recalls living one winter in a tent near the town of Kinlock (near New Kensington) after her father, Diane's maternal grandfather, lost his job in the mines because of his union activities. His life, and his wife's, represented a degree of adversity that would be hardly believable except that it was true. He had fled his native Romania to avoid being inducted into the Austro-Hungarian Army. His wife, also a native Romanian, had been sent to America at the age of thirteen to work as a servant. After his lungs were damaged by battery acid at the Ford assembly plant, he left the comparative security of Detroit's Romanian community, with his wife, to follow work. Diane's mother recalls fleeing the Ku Klux Klan in West

Virginia, where her father had found a job in the coal mines. (This nationwide Klan, distinct in origin from the original Klan, was anti-immigrant and anti-Catholic as well as anti-black.) After her father lost his job at Kinlock, the family was evicted from the company house and was forced to live in a tent before finding an abandoned shanty to live in as the country settled into the Depression. An African-American neighbor helped to sustain them with rabbits and squirrels that she hunted. With factories at full tilt during World War II, he worked two jobs in Pittsburgh, one in a mill, the other in a foundry, for a total of sixteen hours a day. But when the war ended, he found himself unemployed again, and the family returned to the relief rolls until he found a job with Allegheny County which he kept until he retired.

Diane points out that her mother's parents lived outside the kinship networks that were so important to the success of immigrant families here and were cruelly ridiculed for their poverty even by members of other Slavic groups. It was often from an extended family member or a member of the ethnic community that newcomers learned of job openings. Departments in the mills were often given over largely to members of one ethnic group, who solicited new employees from among their own. Families acted as financial and psychological support systems as each member contributed to the survival and well-being of the whole. A person's worth was judged not in terms of individual achievement but in terms of the network of which he was a part. In his essay, "Confessions of a White Ethnic," Michael Novak writes that ethnic people are network people. "Into their definition of themselves," he writes, "enter their family, their in-laws, their relatives, their friends, their streets, their stores, familiar smells and sights and sounds. Those things are not . . . extrinsic. For the network people these things are identity, life, *self*. It is not that the network people are *attached* to such things. They *are* such things."

Diane speaks of the profound and abiding faith of her Croatian grandparents, who were Roman Catholic, and her Romanian grandparents, who were Eastern Orthodox. Her Romanian grandfather remained silent, she says, until he completed his morning prayers. Her great-grandmother and both grandmothers prayed the rosary daily. Food was blessed before eating. She remembers her grandmothers (and her mother, who still does) making the sign of the cross over bread or pie before cutting it. Votive candles burned in the house of her Croatian grandparents. At Epiphany the priest came to bless the house, writing the year and the initials of the three kings over the doorway in chalk.

Saint Nicholas was Diane's Croatian grandparents' church. Diane attended the Saint Nicholas church school through the eighth grade, a nationality school established to perpetuate Croatian culture. At the time, the mass's songs and prayers were offered in Croatian and she attended mass every day. She continued at the school even after the family moved to Stanton Heights, which had an Irish parish. "The family wasn't about to go to an Irish parish," she said, "so I was kept in Saint Nicholas school and the family still went to that church." She remembers certain folk traditions, such as putting silver coins outside the house on New Year's Eve so the family would have money in the New Year. Tradition had it, too, that the first person to cross the threshold of the house in the New Year had to be a dark-haired man, for luck.

Diane's father left high school in the twelfth grade to take a job as a welder, then secured a position at Heppenstall's thanks in part to the recommendation of an uncle. In his off hours he studied engineering and moved to a more skilled position in the mill. In 1969, convinced that the steel industry was facing major changes, he found a civil service job in the Pittsburgh Water Department (this time through the neighborhood network), where he worked his way from stationary engineer to welder to pipe fitter to steam fitter, with each move earning him a better hourly wage.

Diane's mother left high school in the eleventh grade and worked in a box factory and as a domestic. During the 1940s she worked as an operator for Bell Telephone, quitting her job when she married Diane's father. She returned to work once her youngest child was in school, but at first only part-time so that she could manage her responsibilities at home. By the time of her retirement, she had worked for the same company, as a teletypist, a secretary, and a supervisor, for over twenty-seven years.

For her part, like many of her generation, Diane dropped out in her twenties. She stopped going to her church, lost her sense of identity with her religion. "I checked out other churches," she said, "the ones where they sang the 'Hallelujah Chorus' instead of folk songs. The Croatian stuff wasn't that important either." Then in the early 1980s, she was working for a radical, grass-roots law firm that had done some legal work for the *Mill Hunk Herald,* a magazine of blue-collar life and opinion published here from 1979 to 1989. When a play about the Saint Nicholas murals by labor historian David Demarest was performed at the church, one of the church murals appeared on the cover of the *Mill Hunk Herald.* "Here were all these radical politicos at the play about my church," she recalled. "They said to me, 'This is *your* church?!' It made me look at all of it again."

I ask Diane about the advantages and disadvantages of growing up the way she did, how she assesses her early life.

"The plus is the sense of belonging to something," she said, "being part of a community. The minus is that the group doesn't always want to let you go." She still wonders where she got the nerve to quit her secretarial job to go to community college, and then on a scholarship to the University of Pittsburgh. "Blue-collar people weren't raised to go to college," she said. "It wasn't part of the reality. You got a job." When she told her family that she wanted to go to college, they asked her, "What are you going to do with it?" To quit a full-time job with good benefits was foolish. "The parents don't know or understand that network," Diane said, "and there is the fear that their children will outgrow them."

Diane's appreciation of the murals is a blend of family history and her study of Marxist philosophy in college, what she calls her "political awakening." The church is important to her today not so much because she is a "big Catholic," but because it is a link to her heritage. The murals are her family's story, the story of the people she grew up with. She is learning more about her traditions now, coming back to her culture. She says she tried popular culture and it wasn't enough. Her roots have become very special. She is determined not to lose touch with the immigrant experience. She has been so close to it. And it grounds her in this landscape.

The Loss of the Mills

From the vantage point of the 1990s, it seems clear that Big Steel had to almost die. With advances in technology and overcapacity in a global market, no free-market steel industry could continue to support the huge numbers of workers who had depended on it. As I write, the bulk of the area's aging mills have been demolished. In 1984 U.S. Steel closed its Duquesne Works and the remaining steel operations at Clairton, which still operates a coke works. In 1985 LTV Corporation, the corporate successor of Jones & Laughlin, closed all but the coking operation at its historic Pittsburgh Works, and all but a tin mill and a structural mill at its seven-mile-long plant site in Aliquippa. In 1986 U.S. Steel closed its Homestead Works, and Wheeling-Pittsburgh closed its works at Monessen. In 1987, U.S. Steel closed its National Works and sold its Christy Park Works at McKeesport. Many other metals-related plants closed as well, including the American Bridge and Armco plants in Ambridge. Alcoa's New Kensington Works closed even earlier, in 1971. On entering Pittsburgh from the east, one is greeted not by the intricate shapes of Jones & Laughlin's blast furnaces, but by the Pittsburgh Technology Center, a group of modern buildings, lined along the Monongahela in rectangles of lawn, housing such facilities as the University of Pittsburgh Center for Biotechnology & Bioengineering and the Carnegie Mellon Research Institute, which seeks solutions to practical industrial problems. One area of research is devoted to the cleaning of landfills with microwaves.

A development "blueprint" has been proposed for the now vacant site across the river, once the home of the South Side portion of J & L's Pittsburgh Works. Developers are projecting one thousand new housing units, retail stores, parks, warehouse and light industrial space, and facilities for high-tech research and development. Work on roads and on gas, water, sewer, and electric lines is already underway. Upscale housing is projected for the 238-acre slag dump across the Monongahela from Homestead. Hills of slag at Century III Mall are being chewed away by huge earth-moving equipment to be recycled in a multitude of uses. Two high-tech firms have taken space in the newly refurbished machine shop and roll shop buildings at Duquesne. In the meantime, the life of the Edgar Thomson Works in Braddock has been prolonged by the construction of a $250 million continuous slab caster and a $36 million vacuum degasser, which lowers the carbon content of molten steel to give it better "formability." (The construction of a caster was won by the USW as part of the 1986 steel strike settlement.) In Aliquippa, J & L Structural, a steel beam producer not connected with the original J & L, operates out of the 14-inch structural mill bought in 1987 from LTV.

With the convulsions of the 1970s and 1980s behind us, and with the mills largely gone, it is easy to be lulled into the sense that what happened here was part of some natural evolution, some universal law of economics. Old industries give way to new, less advanced technologies to the more sophisticated. It becomes possible to think that it's over now and it *doesn't really matter anymore.* But even if we accept that, as constituted, Big Steel had to almost die, it is clear that the drastic "downsizing" and the near elimination of a one-hundred-year way of life did not have to be so sudden or so brutal. It is also possible that in economic terms the events of the 1980s dealt a blow from which the area will never fully recover.

Seven miles upriver from Pittsburgh, in a great loop of the Monongahela, the boroughs of West Homestead, Homestead, and Munhall (often referred to as a unit simply as Homestead), climb the hillside behind the more than two-mile plat of nearly empty land that was once the Homestead Works of U.S. Steel. I first came to Homestead more than five years ago after reading in *Pittsburgh Magazine* that HAER, the Historic American Engineering Record of the National Park Service, was documenting the mills of the Mon Valley, with an office on Eighth Avenue in Homestead. Unable to find them in the phone book, I simply drove to Homestead and walked up and down the street until I found them. I had never been to Homestead before, but the town's layout and essential identity seemed to match the mill towns, such as Ambridge down the Ohio from Pittsburgh, with which I was more familiar. It was in Homestead that the decline of the steel industry came home to me most potently. At the time, much of the mill remained to be demolished, and the flat land along the river was still clustered with massive, silent plant buildings. I returned often with my camera, recording the progress of demolition, feeling pleasure at the tenacity of a certain foundation that refused to be budged, and sadness at the sight of the truncated entrance ramp at the 48 gate that simply ended in midair, the buildings that one after another simply disappeared. As the rolls of film were finished, I would rush them to a one-hour film processor and wait, eager to have the pictures developed, to have the evidence of the mill buildings in my hand. It was a way of holding on to them.

Now, little on the mill site remains. A dozen stacks, all that is left of the 45-inch slabbing mill, rise from ground level in a solitary line on the West Homestead segment of the site. Upriver, the Homestead High-Level Bridge, on the National Register for the uniqueness of its trusses, delivers traffic from across the river valley. Further upriver, in Munhall, the pump house and water tower, near the site of the Pinkerton landing during the Battle of Homestead, hug the riverbank behind three electric blue plant sheds which have been refurbished and are now "Available." A new Shop 'N Save supermarket, a Rite Aid pharmacy, and a Wendy's are the most notable new presences on what remains for the most part an eerie tabula rasa. (As this book goes to press, there is the possibility that a company making specialty tubes and pipes will move into one of the electric blue buildings.) Frank "Red" Stanford had been superintendent of the 45-inch mill for eleven years when he retired in 1972. "When I pulled out of the mill for the last time," he said, "I wondered to myself what would be here in a hundred years. Now it's only twenty-five years and it's all gone." Recently, plans were announced by the Park Corporation, which now owns the site, for ambitious new development that would include a huge multiscreen theater, restaurants, retail stores, offices, and upscale apartments, as well as bike paths and a marina. But the question remains whether the development, even if it comes to fruition, can ever generate the jobs and well-being, the sense of identity, once provided by the mill.

With the demolition of the mill, the land of "the Ward" is doubly vacant. Actually two wards and parts of two more, this land below the tracks, covering the area from First Avenue to

Sixth, had housed, among others, the "Slavs" described by Margaret Byington in her volume of the Pittsburgh Survey. With the beginning of World War II the area was targeted for demolition: two thousand homes, eleven churches, two convents, five schools, countless groceries and other shops, twenty-eight taverns, and twelve social clubs, pulled down by the Defense Plant Corporation to allow for expansion of the mill, and in particular its armor plate capacity for battleships and destroyers. Only Russian (Rusin) Hall on what was then Fourth Avenue was spared, to be used as a meeting and conference facility by the mill. To outsiders the area was a slum. To many who lived there it was a close-knit community of lifelong neighbors, a rich ethnic mix. In a videotape produced in 1989 by the Historical Society of Western Pennsylvania before the mill was demolished, one former ward resident expressed the bond he still felt to his former home: "I have a good idea where my house was," he said. "I hope they won't tear down all the furnaces, but I'm sure a great deal will be torn down. And I'm going to walk back there. . . . I know that when I hit that spot, I will not need a surveyor's transit to tell me where the house was. I think my heart will tell me at that moment that I'm standing, standing right there on the house site."

As I stroll, parallel to the mill site, on Eighth Avenue, the boroughs' main commercial street, I can still see the marks of a multiethnic steel town. Ingot molds stand on an ingot buggy across from the mouth of the Homestead High-Level Bridge and from Chiodo's Tavern, a local landmark crammed with memorabilia, established in 1890. An advertisement for Great American Federal Savings and Loan, once the Slovak bank, covers one of Chiodo's exterior sidewalls. On the other sidewall a sign reads "Welcome to the Former Steel Capital of the World." Some fraternal lodges remain: the Bulgaro-Macedonian

Beneficial Association, Owl's Club 1538, Moose Lodge 60, and the Homestead Slavs just off the avenue.

The signs on the shopfronts of the turn-of-the-century commercial buildings show a mix of past and present: Lucci's Market, Bubba's Lounge (closed), Levine Brothers Hardware, Lapko's Bar and Grill, Amos Supermarket (closed), Steel Valley Cards, Video Rentals, Used Book Store, Rainbow Kitchen and Health Center, a men's clothing store, and, typical of the steel towns, as well as city neighborhoods, at least one columned granite branch of a bank. An ornate building with a balustraded facade houses Homestead Business Machines. The Tindall Building, built in 1895, has undergone a stylish renovation by the Homestead Area Economic Revitalization Corporation. A federal grant has provided funds for new trees, streetlamps, and signs. When I first came to Homestead I felt I had stepped back in time at Moxley's Drug Store, with its sort of Tyrolean gingerbread exterior, its glass-doored display cabinets, its tin ceiling, and its soda fountain and stools. The space is empty now and available for rent.

Former skilled-worker housing rises above me up the hillside, avenue after avenue of sturdy brick houses with porches and hipped or gable roofs. Many have enviable interior woodwork. A statue of the Virgin graces several front lawns. Walking along the sidewalks I feel an aura of neighborliness, though too many of the houses have become shabby. A more spacious house on Eleventh Avenue, one of a number built in the area for mill superintendents, boasts a leaded-glass window on the second floor in which blast furnace stoves glow orange against the gray of other plant buildings. It is an area punctuated by churches. From the intersection of Tenth and Ann there are sixteen churches within eyeshot: Lutheran, Methodist, Roman Catholic, Presbyterian, A.M.E., Russian Orthodox, Hungarian Reformed, the former Byzantine Rite Cathedral of Saint John the Baptist, and more. The cathedral, built in 1903 to serve Slovaks, Carpatho-Rusyns, and Hungarians, is now the East European Cultural Center. The Community of the Crucified One occupies a former synagogue. Many of the churches show the mark of working people. The figure of Saint Joseph the Worker stands over sculpted vessels of molten steel above the tower of the Slovak Saint Michael's Roman Catholic Church. (Saint Michael appears over the main portal.) The onion domes of Saint Nicholas Russian Orthodox Church and the steeple of the First Hungarian Reformed Church are plated with stainless steel rolled at the Homestead Works.

The parishioners of Saint Mary Magdalene Roman Catholic Church have recently met a challenge from the head of the Pittsburgh diocese, Bishop Donald Wuerl. Dwindling population had necessitated an areawide consolidation of parishes, but their church would not be closed if they could raise the more than $350,000 needed for repairs. The current Romanesque structure with its two imposing towers had been rebuilt after a fire during the Depression with, as in the case of so many of the area's churches, the dimes and quarters of its parishioners. One pair of round-arched, stained-glassed windows shows a farmer with his scythe, a laborer with his shovel, an artisan at his forge, in deep blues, scarlet, flesh tones, and flashes of yellow gold. After dozens of fundraising events, from bake sales to Homestead area church and house tours, the parishioners had raised the necessary funds, and in 1996 the repairs were completed. But the newspaper account of the church's rededication ends with a telling irony. The granddaughter of one of the fundraising leaders would soon be baptized at the church, in perhaps the first baptism since the refurbishing. Her parents, however, do not live in Homestead. The baby, the article read, would be "driven in from New Jersey for the event."

In Frick Park, on Tenth Avenue across from Saint Mary's, are the remains of a war memorial, a curving wall engraved with the words "To Those Who Served." On one of my first trips to Homestead, I sat on a low portion of wall that completes the enclosure, struck by the gamut of names listed on the central marker, names like: Adams, Butka, Cohen, Dubravski, Erbeck, Flaherty, Forbes, Gentile, Gudzinas, Konstandinos, Kozak, Margolis, McAllister, Navjokaitis, Rizzio, Rogers, Saska, Schwartz, Vebelunas, Yakubansky, Zidow. The marker has since been removed to a site near Chiodo's and the Homestead High-Level Bridge. "People were writing all over it, defacing it," the Homestead borough secretary's office told me. The flat rectangle of its foundation is all that remains.

A few blocks up the avenue, the massive, nearly block-long Carnegie Library of Homestead reigns over its portion of hillside. The third of Carnegie's libraries, it is built of dun-colored brick and at its opening housed showers and bathtubs, a swimming pool, a billiard room, bowling alleys, an exercise room, a basketball court, and a music hall, as well as reading rooms and stacks. In concluding his speech at its dedication six years after the Homestead Strike, Carnegie enjoined his audience to "Take . . . this building as the gift of one workman to other workmen," neglecting the fact that many of his workmen labored such long hours they would scarcely have the time or energy to take advantage of it. Carnegie would now be able to forget the events of the Homestead Strike. That "deplorable event," he said, speaking of himself and his wife, had not even yet "lost its power at intervals to sadden our lives." Further up the hillside, workers who had died in the strike lay, past protest, in their unmarked graves. But the sight of his audience, their welcome and their "smiling faces" would banish "all the regretful thoughts, all the unpleasant memories."

According to Doris Dyen of the Steel Industry Heritage Corporation, Eastern Europeans in Homestead are an aging population now, a population of those near retirement when the mills went down, who owned their own houses and couldn't afford to buy new, and younger families of workers who couldn't retrain, people who haven't been able to make it and couldn't leave to make it somewhere else. (Income levels in West Homestead and lower Munhall are slightly higher than Homestead proper; those in upper Munhall, Twentieth Avenue and above, higher still.) African Americans, many of them displaced by urban renewal in Pittsburgh during the 1960s and 1970s, have seen their jobs in the mill or their small businesses—shoeshine shops, taverns, and other establishments—dry up with the loss of the mill. "Homestead right now, that's a bad name," Leonard Fleming told me. "People don't want to come in. It's a shame, and you say to yourself, 'How long?'"

The painter Robert Qualters has a studio, up two long flights of stairs, on the third floor of a building at the corner of East Eighth Avenue and Ann Street. Bob is one of the first people I met here after my return and a good friend. We have formed the habit of having lunch together every few weeks, and I stop by his studio to pick him up when we are to have lunch in Homestead. Dressed typically in safari shirt and canvas trousers, he is a sturdy man with wavy gray hair and eyes that shine with a gentle, jolly irreverence. His studio is alive with shapes and colors set off against white walls—paintings, panel fragments, studies for larger work. Bob was born in McKeesport, and grew up there and in Clairton. He has tried other places, such as Berkeley, where he lived while studying with Richard Diebenkorn. But he came home. I asked him why. "I don't know," he said with a smile. "I tried to paint in California, but the light just didn't feel right."

I have two of Bob's paintings in my living room, one a rain-drenched, Impressionist landscape, veiled with melancholy, of OH 5 at Homestead, the eleven-furnace open hearth facility built during World War II, being dismembered by the fire of a demolition crew's torch. The other is of skyscrapers in down-town Pittsburgh, all vibrant line, suffused with a sunlike yel-low light. A winged chrysalis, merely suggested amid the build-ings' lines, swirls toward the sky.

Working with an assistant, artist Sharon Spell, Bob has produced a series of images honoring Homestead's heritage. Early in 1996, ten years after the Homestead Works was closed, his panels were hung like banners from new lampposts, riv-eted I-beams painted a deep forest green, along East Eighth Avenue. In technique the paintings show a softness of color and line that, for me, bespeak affection. As in a museum, au-diotapes expanding on the images will one day be available to visitors.

The subjects of the panels create a time capsule of Home-stead's cultural and economic history, a series of highlights glimpsed in a walk up the street: ethnic folk dancers, women making pierogies, the wide expanse of the High-Level Bridge emptying into the streets of Homestead, the Carnegie library, onion domes, gospel singers, the Leona Theater, and the Home-stead Grays. The renowned Negro League team was owned by Cumberland Posey, son of the founder of the Black Diamond Coke and Coal Company, once the largest black-owned busi-ness in the area. The Leona Theater opened as the Stahl The-ater in 1925 at a cost of one million dollars, a fabulous sum at the time. It had a seating capacity of over eighteen hundred people and brought in such vaudeville stars as Sophie Tucker and George Burns and Gracie Allen, as well as the latest films. Closed in 1966, the landmark building was used occasionally for special events—rock concerts, magic shows, plays—until it was torn down in 1983. It was replaced by a gas station and convenience store.

Other panels celebrate the mill: glowing ladles suspended on crane hooks, a bank of open hearths, the familiar arch reading "Homestead USS Steel Works" over the Amity Street gate. *Mill Workers 1895* shows three mustachioed, presumably Eastern European workers, in felt hats, one in a vest with shirtsleeves rolled, each holding a pickax, the tool of his labor. *Homestead Works—1905* looks down on dense rows of plant sheds and billowing stacks. *The Hole in the Wall,* the legendary mill entrance gate at City Farm Lane, was literally a hole in a wall which housed the office of the paymaster. The entrance was notorious in earlier decades for the legions that congregated outside: gypsies, prostitutes, injured workers seeking a handout, and wives trying to intercept their husbands' paychecks before they were consumed at a nearby tavern. Recent efforts by local historians to save the Hole in the Wall were rebuffed by the Park Corporation, and in 1993 the wall was torn down.

Another panel, 48" *Universal Mill,* portrays the gargantuan 48-inch universal plate rolling mill, the last steam-powered mill in the United States. Installed in 1899 and shut down in 1979, it produced steel plate from ten inches to forty-eight inches wide, and up to 120 feet long. Thicknesses ranged from one-quarter of an inch to fifteen inches. The noise of its great steam engine, 5,820 horsepower, was audible ten miles away. Its crankshaft alone weighed twenty-four tons. Old-timers recall the mill's vibrations shaking the shanties across the street, the blasts, like thunder, resonating from the building's inte-

111

rior. Salt was thrown on the hot plates as they went back and forth through the rolls to break the scale that had formed on the surface of the slab. The compression of salt, scale, and water (sprayed on the plates to wash off the debris), resulted in a series of short, deafening booms. "The compression, awhhh, you talk about fireworks," exclaimed Leonard Fleming, who worked in the mill for forty-two years. "Boom, boom, boom, boom. You could hear it all the way up on Whitaker Hill. That compression in there with that salt, the water, and the scale. That scale would shoot off the plates. It flew all over the place.

"Sometimes," he added, "when a visitor came into the mill, that gauger would throw extra salt on." He makes the sound of an explosion, then smiles mischievously. "It shook the dirt from the rafters!"

I asked Leonard if he had felt excited about the mill and what it could do. "Oh, yes," he said. "Considering the age of that mill, you would take a little piece of steel, seventy-two inches long and, let's say, twenty-four inches wide by seven inches thick, and you would elongate that to about twelve hundred to fourteen hundred inches long. And you would see that steel elongated out, longer and longer and longer and longer. It was amazing."

In late 1990 and early 1991, Steel Industry Heritage Task Force contractors and volunteers, overseen by experts in the preservation of industrial machinery, dismantled and cataloged the mill. Its aggregate nine hundred tons of machinery and equipment was first documented by historians, photographers, and architects from HAER, then cleaned of a hundred years' worth of rust and grime. Industrial riggers needed three months to dismantle and remove the machinery, the pieces of which now number in the thousands. In November 1996, seven counties in southwestern Pennsylvania were declared a national heritage area, the result of continuing efforts by the Steel Industry Heritage Corporation (called the Steel Industry Heritage Task Force until 1991) to preserve the story of Big Steel in a series of river sites. It is hoped that the mill will one day be reassembled in a museum proposed for the Carrie Furnace site in Rankin, across the river from Homestead. Two of the complex of furnaces that once smelted ore for the Homestead Works still stand there, unused.

Another of Qualters's panels, *Changing Shifts*, recalls the great tide of workers pouring into the mill, flowing out, part of the rhythm of a mill town's days and nights. Bob's image shows two workers, one black, one white, reaching out to one another as they part amidst the crowd. Although based on an actual photograph taken in 1960, the panel is optimistic in its suggestion that blacks and whites were on equal footing in the mill. Blacks were indeed represented in the steel industry, but they tended to hold the dirtiest, meanest, and least rewarding jobs, what many referred to as "nigger jobs," with little chance for advancement until the Consent Decree of 1974, in which nine major steel companies and the United Steelworkers of America agreed to provide equal opportunities to minorities and women. I think of Patricia Dobler's poem "Steelmark Day Parade, 1961," in which the poet's "dark-haired visitor" asks, "But really, where *are* the Negroes?"

"Not here, not yet," the poet replies, "they don't exist in 1961."

Mill Worker 1975 shows a young woman in hard hat and safety glasses, holding a gauge that measures slabs, testimony to the agreement of the previous year. Only within the context of manpower shortages during World War II had women been previously employed on the mill floor.

In *Homestead Works—1985*, plant buildings hug the curving bank of the river in a valley of verdant hills. The scene is calm. There is no smoke. The Homestead Works had made steel for such emblematic American structures as the Flatiron Building, the Empire State Building, the Panama Canal, the United Nations Building, the George Washington Bridge, and San Francisco's Bay Bridge. But by 1985 it was nearly over. Within a year the last of the mill's departments would shut down.

When Nikita Khrushchev came to the United States in 1959, he was intent on seeing what he considered the defining elements of America, among them a farm and a steel mill. They brought him to Homestead, though not to the Homestead Works, which had been shut down by a nationwide steel strike, but to the Mesta Machine works in West Homestead, manufacturers of steel mill machinery and, incidentally, the source of the fortune that fueled the career of international hostess Perle Mesta. The George and Perle Mesta house, with its adjacent ballroom (where her career began), still stands partway up the hill at 540 Doyle Avenue in West Homestead.

The 1950s were heady days in Homestead. The mill was running full out, feeding the postwar demand for automobiles and other consumer goods, housing, and infrastructure. Crowds thronged Eighth Avenue, with its some three hundred stores, day and night. There was money to spend: on automobiles, maybe even a boat, the good life—bars, music, sporting events, the movies, and more dubious attractions like gambling and prostitution, though after a crackdown by local authorities the latter were on the decline. "In its heyday Eighth Avenue was like Broadway," Frank Stanford said. "It was lighted twenty-four hours a day. Homestead was booming." Leonard Fleming said much the same: "Homestead was a meeting place for everybody," he recalled. "If you wanted to come down Saturday night and you wanted to see somebody, you'd come down Eighth Avenue and you'd run into them sooner or later." Braddock, McKeesport, Duquesne, Aliquippa—mill towns up and down the rivers bustled with the fruits of a nearly middle-class life. Many families moved further up the hill to Upper Munhall or to such blue-collar suburbs as West Mifflin. With the growth of the United Steelworkers of America, which began in 1936 as the Steel Workers Organizing Committee (SWOC), with headquarters in downtown Pittsburgh, workers, it seemed, had secured a base that would ensure a fairer share of the wealth that they and their fathers and their grandfathers had helped to create.

The trouble was that, in a single-industry town, life was necessarily dependent on the mill. For many the pull of the mill was irresistible: good wages without the need for higher education, a settled life in a pattern set over generations, a life in which people knew what to expect and knew what was expected of them. Poet and former steelworker Peter Blair writes that "at one point in the 1950s over 4,000 men out of approximately 10,000 in the Homestead Works were father-son combinations."

"It was so easy just to roll down the hill into work at the mill," said Randolph Harris, historian, photographer, and former community organizer for the Steel Industry Heritage Task Force.

Mill and municipality became inextricably intertwined. In Homestead, steel company crews cleaned the streets, maintained the library, fabricated bearings for church bells, among a multitude of services. Managers loaned cranes and other heavy equipment. "Up here on Ravine Street," Leonard Fleming recalled, "the bridge washed out and they needed beam. They made a phone call and the mill sent a beam up there. No ifs, ands, or buts. If there was something going on and somebody needed a trophy or something, a lot of them was made in the machine shop." All at company expense. Real estate taxes on mill property constituted a major portion of the tax base. Schools were geared toward producing good steelworkers. The mill was the touchstone, the constant. There were downturns, there were layoffs and strikes. It was a cyclical business. "One year you'd go out and buy a new car," said steelworker and artist Tom Dawson, "and the next year you could hardly pay for it. That's the way the steel business was."

For a while it was all too easy. As orders poured in, management simply raised prices to cover wage and benefit increases negotiated with the union. Union leaders were satisfied with their role simply as negotiators, leaving ideas for improving plant operations up to the company. Within fifteen years of its formation the union was becoming as much a bureaucracy as the corporation, unresponsive to the rank and file and fiercely resistant to new ideas or challenges from its membership.

But lack of vision and satisfaction with the status quo were not the province of union management alone. As steelmaking capacity expanded globally after World War II, U.S. steelmakers, satisfied with the tonnage they were producing and reluctant to abandon their already huge capital investments, stayed with familiar technologies, leaving research and the implementation of more advanced technologies largely to others. The basic oxygen furnace, for example, a significant advance over the open hearth, was first used in Austria in the early 1950s. When the U.S. steel industry began its shift to the BOP in the 1960s it was already too late.

New investment, when it did come, was haphazard. A state-of-the-art rolling mill, built at Duquesne in the late 1950s, was intended to keep the works in operation for years to come. But the company did not build a continuous caster, the technology for which was established by the mid-1960s, and the mill became out of date. Homestead got a stainless steel facility in 1969, but only Duquesne, and later E.T., got a basic oxygen furnace. "The general superintendent who was liked downtown [at U.S. Steel headquarters] got whatever he wanted," Manny Stoupis said to me. "But there was no planning. There was lots of good stuff but not in one place." Profits were kept high by emphasizing quantity, that is, high production, at the expense of quality.

Careless cost controls allowed for flagrant overmanning and extensive pilfering. A friend of mine commented on the summer job he held at Aliquippa when he was in college. "I got a lot of books read," he said. The tradition of "getting it at the mill," an outgrowth, probably, of the company's doing for the towns, was rampant, as items ranging from toilet paper to tools—wrenches, sockets, saws, drills—to light fixtures, to brass gears and couplings went over the fence or out the gate. Another friend remembers a worker who rolled a two-foot spool of copper cable to the fence, put one end through a hole, and circled around outside the fence to pull the five-hundred feet of cable through. White-collar workers were as guilty as blue-collar, filching office supplies, using company crews and materials to make home improvements, playing golf.

In the context of overmanning, former workers speak of having "slowed down" so as to leave some work for the next shift. The mills operated under the rigid system of work rules that finally acted as a barrier for workers to hide behind in their dealings with management. Corporation executives had not ceased to regard the workers as a mass of faceless individuals whose job was to follow orders. In response, workers felt little inclined to find ways to make the mills more efficient, or when the time came, to accept wage cuts or work rule reform. (In the end it would be E.T. and not Duquesne that survived, largely because its local was ultimately willing to make greater concessions.)

In 1973, the corporations and the union reached an Experimental Negotiating Agreement (ENA), designed to eliminate national strikes. Strikes resulted in hedge buying by customers as union contracts were about to expire and an increased reliance on foreign steel to ensure an uninterrupted supply. The agreement provided for automatic annual pay increases of at least 3 percent, along with cost-of-living adjustments that rose with the period's often soaring inflation. The agreement also left rigid work rules largely in place, making improvements in productivity nearly impossible without simply closing an entire plant. Ultimately, negotiations in 1974, 1977, and 1980 were governed by the agreement.

By the time Big Steel removed its blinders the world had drastically changed. In 1946, the United States produced 54.1 percent of the world's raw steel. By the 1960s Japanese and European firms were moving steel into the United States. By 1970 the U.S. share of the world market was down to 20.1 percent, by 1980 to 14 percent. In the same year Japan's share was 16 percent. In 1984 the United States accounted for 11.8 percent of the world's steel production. By that time, the U.S. industry was also threatened by new steel industries in such developing countries as Taiwan, South Korea, and Brazil, whose low labor and material costs, modern equipment, and governmental support put them at a competitive advantage in a global market. The high value of the dollar at the time only compounded the domestic industry's disadvantage, making imports less expensive and U.S. exports more so. By 1986 there was a global overcapacity of two hundred million tons.

Two other major factors had a deleterious effect on Big Steel's market: the increasing use of competing materials and the growth of the minimills. Plastic and fiberglass supplanted a significant portion of the steel used by the automobile industry; aluminum substituted for steel in beverage cans. At the same time, the market share of the domestic minimills, specializing in such products as rod and wire and small bars, had increased to 18 percent by 1982. The minimills were more cost-effective primarily because of their use of continuous casters, their elimination of the blast furnace process, and their work force, which is nonunion. Richard Preston, author of *American Steel*, points out that by decade's end one company alone, Nucor, had taken a billion dollars' worth of steel markets from Big Steel. (More recently, the firm has been investing in so-called thin slab casters which streamline the manufacture of sheet steel, the last main province of the big integrated steel companies.)

Big Steel was handicapped by the very integration that had proved so effective in earlier decades. By the 1950s, for example, the high-grade ores of the Mesabi Range, long a major source of ore for the big steel companies, had run out. U.S. firms invested heavily in Canadian ore fields and in plants designed to upgrade and pelletize low-grade ores, thereby locking themselves into higher costs, rather than take advantage of high-grade ores from Australia and Brazil that were often less expensive, but over which they would have less control.

Contrary to the repeated rosy predictions of economic prognosticators, Big Steel had been on shaky ground for some time. As William Serrin writes in *Homestead: The Glory and Tragedy of an American Steel Town,* "Had it not been for military production in World War II, the Korean War, and Vietnam, and guaranteed production from such projects as the expressway system and airports, the corporation [U.S. Steel], likely would have fallen years before." When the situation reached crisis proportions the company blamed imports, environmental controls, high labor costs, anything but themselves. More carefully considered long-range planning and a more informed response to world markets might have led to gradual streamlining, rendering eventual cataclysm unnecessary. Neither management nor union rose to the occasion. With capital investments in the aging mills written off, it was cheaper for the corporation to increase employment during periods of higher demand, and to lay off workers during market downturns, rather than invest in newer technologies and be forced to negotiate with the union over the potential loss of jobs. After earning a profit of $242,000,000 in 1978, U.S. Steel lost $293,000,000 in 1979 and a staggering $561,700,000 in the fourth quarter of 1980. U.S. Steel had already closed some forty plants between 1974 and 1979, including Open Hearth No. 4 and the 48-inch universal mill at Homestead. That was nothing compared to what was to come. By 1982, the steel industry was operating at little more than 30 percent of its capacity; approximately twenty thousand steelworkers in the Mon Valley were laid off. In March of that year, after receiving investment tax credits it claimed were necessary to modernize the mills, U.S. Steel bought Marathon Oil for over six billion dollars instead. In December, the company announced that it would close the remaining Carrie Furnaces and Open Hearth No. 5, built during the mill expansion of World War II. Plant by plant, department by department, Big Steel was being eviscerated. Pittsburgh's corporate leaders voiced no protest. The consensus was that Pittsburgh should become a more diversified, white-collar town.

"In closing plants and terminating workers," Serrin writes, "the corporation acted in a most arrogant and imperious manner. It made announcements around the holidays. Executives never went into the communities to attempt to explain decisions. Often union officials would receive no official notification but instead would receive a telephone call just before an announcement, or read rumors in a newspaper or hear them on the radio or television." John Hoerr, author of *And the Wolf Finally Came,* a landmark account of the decline of the steel industry, said much the same. "From 1981 on," he wrote, "U.S. Steel acted with a callousness that will not soon be forgotten. The economics of the world steel trade dictated that the corporation shut down plants and reduce its work force. There was no pleasant way to do that. U.S. Steel, however, seemed to go out of its way to turn unpleasantness into nasty displays of power." (Hoerr does add that U.S. Steel paid out enormous sums of money in the form of pension and medical benefits to recipients in the Mon Valley.)

A number of grass roots organizations sprang up in response, union activists allied with various churches, with goals and tactics ranging from the constructive to the incendiary, and self-defeating. The Mon Valley Unemployed Committee dedicated itself most directly to the survival of the individual steelworker in the establishment of food banks, the prevention of mortgage foreclosures and utility shutoffs, and assistance in applying for food stamps and welfare or collecting unemployment compensation. The far more notorious Denominational Ministry Strategy, or DMS, a group of Protestant clergymen allied with a small group of union members called the Network to Save the Mon-Ohio Valley, attacked the Pittsburgh power structure itself. Forms of protest included spraying skunk oil in Mellon Bank branches or placing dead fish in safe deposit boxes. The targeting of Mellon was understandable. In February 1983, Mellon had foreclosed on Mesta Machine and frozen its accounts, leaving Mesta employees unpaid for work already performed. Soon after, it was revealed that Mellon had over $100 million invested in Sumitomo Industries of Japan, Mesta's principal competitor. When challenged publicly, Mellon's CEO claimed to see nothing wrong in favoring foreign jobs over local if the bank's investment brought a higher return.

Network/DMS activists also carried their message to the churches of Pittsburgh's corporate elite, most frequently to Shadyside Presbyterian, the church of top Mellon and U.S. Steel executives and one of the historic congregations of the Pittsburgh establishment. A plaque in the north transept of the massive stone building commemorates "the first radio message broadcast to the arctic regions." The message was sent from the church through Westinghouse station KDKA and received by the Hudson Bay Company on Christmas Sunday evening, 1922. Three protesters in ski masks burst in on the church's Christmas party in 1984 and threw balloons filled with water and skunk oil at church members, including children. On Easter Sunday 1985, demonstrators marched toward the church with boxes of metal scrap to lay at the altar, carrying a banner that read: "All We Have, Scraps of Mills." Their leaders were arrested at the church's property line. Even today the mention of Network/DMS tactics brings frowns to the faces of many who were otherwise sympathetic, for their betrayal of the Pittsburgh Renaissance tradition and the city's basic civility, and for their lack of regard for women and children and the sanctity of the church. The tactics have been attributed to

Charles Honeywell, an outside organizer schooled in the methods of Saul Alinsky and hired by the DMS. But it must also be said that people may take desperate measures when they are fighting for their lives.

Awash in the tide of plant closings, hopes merged, if only briefly, in the figure of a blast furnace, in the campaign to save the Duquesne Works' Dorothy Six. The largest blast furnace in the valley, twenty-eight stories high, with a hearth measuring twenty-eight feet in diameter, Dorothy was only twenty-one years old when she was shut down in the spring of 1984. A plan to acquire Dorothy as a worker-owned facility, along with Duquesne's basic oxygen shop and the primary mill, which would roll ingots into semifinished slabs, had been proposed by Local 1256 president Mike Bilcsik and the Tri-State Conference on Steel, a nonprofit organization dedicated to preserving and reopening manufacturing plants in western Pennsylvania, eastern Ohio, and northern West Virginia. U.S. Steel executives, who had announced that they would tear down Duquesne's "hot end," were irritated by this challenge to their judgment, but allowed a preliminary study funded by the USW, Allegheny County, and the City of Pittsburgh to proceed.

Of primary importance was to prevent irreparable physical damage to Dorothy in the cold winter months to come. Local 1256 members raised the four thousand dollars needed for antifreeze and other materials and the sixteen thousand dollars demanded by U.S. Steel for insurance and donated their labor to winterize the furnace. When the results of the study were announced, the valley was jubilant. Here it seemed was a possible triumph of David over Goliath, a symbol of promise far outweighing the number of jobs involved. It would take an estimated $90 million to restart the furnace but the proposed operation could net $35 million within three years. Construction of a continuous caster, if deemed desirable, would cost an additional $150 million. U.S. Steel moved immediately to debunk the report, but also agreed to delay demolition while further studies were conducted. Workers took no chances. Parking a trailer they dubbed "Fort Duquesne" across from the plant's main gate, two hundred laid-off steelworkers set up a round-the-clock vigil, in a curious echo of "Fort Frick" and the Homestead Strike, to prevent the company from sending in demolition crews.

But the plan was not to be. A subsequent study by Lazard Frères, with which U.S. Steel cooperated, determined that the plan was indeed unworkable without the construction of a continuous caster that would produce the higher quality slabs the market now demanded. Financing would "not be forthcoming from the private capital markets." Furthermore, U.S. Steel had made their intentions clear. Not only would they not cooperate with the mill were it to reopen, they would, in the words of Mike Locker, author of the original study, "throw everything they had at it to compete with it." And so the project, and the hopes of the valley, died.

Wes Slusher worked in the blast furnace accounting office at Duquesne from September 1956 to June 1984. He is proud of his work record, first as safety clerk, then as incentive clerk, and finally as production statistical clerk. From November 1960 to December 1976 he "never lost a day's pay." In his diary/scrapbook of his time in the mill, he recalls the nationwide, 116-day steel strike of 1959, during which he received no unemployment compensation, no help from the union. "That strike put me in the hole for years," he says.

Slusher was the last regular employee at the blast furnace, closing out statistical reports and calculating incentive pay for the production workers. During his final week, he was alone in the office and would slip out to wander among and photograph the mill structures.

"We broke every production record [with Dorothy] in 1983," he writes, "and got the Ironmaster Award." Workers were stunned when U.S. Steel chairman David Roderick announced in December that the steelmaking facilities at Duquesne would be closed. "In 1984, the men again broke every production record," Slusher wrote, "hoping that Roderick would change his mind. You could see the fear and desperation in their eyes."

In his scrapbook Slusher includes a copy of a letter from general foreman Manny Stoupis written to the men and women of No. 6 blast furnace after Roderick's announcement. "Today," Stoupis wrote, "word was received that at the end of May, #6 Blast Furnace will be blown down. I don't think anything has hurt as much—I couldn't believe it either. . . . I spoke to many of you on Tuesday evening because I wanted you to know that losing our furnace is tough, but *if* we go down, losing you people will be the toughest part of all. You have been the finest group of individuals anyone could work with. Your efforts in our three year association are known nationwide, you all have made blast furnace history."

As the month of May, and shutdown, approached, Slusher waited for some form of congratulations from the company and the union, some form of thanks. But, he says, "None came."

At 11:25 A.M. on May 24, 1984, Dorothy was shut down. Workers wore black arm bands and tried to hold back tears. Bob Macey was a fourth-generation worker at Duquesne, his father, grandfather, and great-grandfather having worked there before him. On his final shift, the sixteen-year veteran of the mill, age thirty-five, played Taps over the plant's public address system. From above Dorothy was filled with gravel, then

125

casted until it could be determined that the gravel was down. Then she was shut down.

A snapshot in Slusher's scrapbook shows an open locker crammed with jacket, boots, slicker, jeans, and myriad other personal items. Slusher's caption reads: "The man who used this locker came back . . . at the end of his shift, knew it was his last day, looked at what was inside, said 'Fuck it' and walked away."

"When I came to work in 1956," Slusher wrote of the blast furnace department, "we had 6 furnaces working 24 hours a day, and employed over 1,000 men. To walk through that area, seeing no people, hearing no sound, was to be the loneliest experience of my life. As I walked past Dorothy furnace for the last time, I said 'Good By Dorothy.'"

Before leaving the mill, Slusher stopped to shake hands with people in the few mill departments still operating. Then, with his personal items under his arm, he walked out the gate. "What the hell," he asked himself, "am I going to do now?"

"When Dorothy went down," Manny Stoupis recalled, "I had a foreman come to me and we embraced and we both started bawling, and he says to me, 'Boss, we did everything you asked us to do and now we don't have a job anymore.' He said, 'Manny, we did it all. Why are we going down?' And that was the truth. I didn't have an answer for him. The corporation didn't have the guts to come in and tell those people why.

"It's like seeing people die in battle," Manny said. "These guys did their all for me and I'll never forget that. I had a job. I knew I was going to E.T. But how do you turn away a bunch of guys who gave you their all?"

In the early 1980s, an anonymous survey of unemployed steelworkers in Chicago asked the question "What have been the worst effects of you being unemployed on you and your family?" As part of his "Home Scrap" project, documenting the decline of the steel industry, the artist Raymon Elozua superimposed reproductions of the survey's handwritten replies onto photographic portraits, "found images," of anonymous steelworkers from books and other materials on the industry. The text of one worker's reply read as follows: "Being out of work has hurt me and my family great dearly I cannot find work and it very hard and sad It like a bad dream every thing has gone wrong in my life. I am just barely holding on to life I stay very sad nowday because I cannot find a job It like a curse Please help me.' Before it too late."

The response is written in mostly block letters, on lined paper. The last two sentences have been crossed out.

Another responded, "There is no money, my spouse has supported the house hold since my layoff and ran out of unemployment funds, there is no extra money, no extra food, and 1 car sold, no vacation or any other luxytry, I have been seeking a job since my lay off with no luck every place you go it's no work, no jobs, or we're not hiring maybe later."

Another's handwritten response:

> LOS$ OF HOME
> LOS$ OF WIFE + FAMILY
> LOSS OF FRIENDS
> LOSS OF SELF-RESPECT, + ESTEEM
> DEPRESSION + ANGER
> FEELINGS OF HOPELESSNESS

Pittsburgh poet Patricia Dobler grew up in Middletown, Ohio, where Armco Steel had a major presence. She speaks almost with wonder of the image of her father, then retired, "a big German man," proud of his life in the mill, standing in his driveway with tears streaming down his face on learning that

127

the mill was cutting back and his son was out of a job. His son, Dobler's brother, representing the fourth generation of the family at the mill, felt the loss of his job as not unlike the rejection of a father, so benevolent had been the mill's particular brand of paternalism. Workers and their families were losing not merely a job but a multigenerational way of life. It was "like losing your family tree," said Bob Macey, the worker who played Taps at the shutdown of Dorothy Six. Security had been part of the bargain the steelworker had struck, accepting the rigors and limitations of the mill for stability, a good wage, and the familiarity and continuity of home. Out of the industry of the valley, came, in the words of the writer David Walton, "not an enrichment, but a congruence to daily life, so that people living there now have to feel a vacuum."

In a sense steelworkers were losing their identity, their understanding of their place in the world. Even the most humble had been able to see their contribution in buildings, bridges, cars, ships. At the same time, the identity they were losing was part of the difficulty in starting over. Trained only as steelworkers, their skills not necessarily transferable to other jobs, they were often seen as underqualified and, for members of the union, too accustomed to being overpaid. Some men, ashamed that they were no longer the breadwinner, refused to answer the phone during the day while their wives were at work. Money worries and the stress of changing roles led to an increase in the divorce rate. A few men took their own lives.

I remember the waitress in the lunchroom at E.T., a woman in her sixties, in a pink uniform, removing dishes from the empty tables. Her father had been gassed at a blast furnace at Homestead in 1945. As I waited to tour the new continuous caster, we spoke of the 1980s and the disintegration of her neighborhood.

"The valley has been through a lot," I said to her.

"Too much, honey," she replied, her voice little more than a whisper. "Too much."

Still, most soldiered on, sending out resumes, picking up odd jobs until permanent (and probably lower paying) employment could be found. Ken Johnston spoke of delivering resumes to the north one day, to the west the next. "I'd take maybe Monday and go north. Everything between here and New Castle. Tuesday I'd go south. I'd just go along the parkway and start pulling over everywhere possible and start handing out my resumes." He averaged three forays a week over a period of two years.

Meanwhile, the tax base of the mill towns was decimated. Assessed values of mill sites were drastically reduced. As much as 20 percent of the housing stock in Homestead was abandoned in 1991. For a while the borough of West Homestead was playing the lottery. Drugs and gang-related violence became commonplace. Recently, Homestead's mayor journeyed to Washington seeking funds to staff an adequate, full-time police force.

Some persisted in believing, before they were demolished, that the mills would eventually come back. The steel business was cyclical, after all, and there had been other downturns. I could understand the feeling. I often drove past the remaining plant buildings of J & L's South Side works after my return to Pittsburgh and was always particularly struck by one looming exterior wall that pressed close against the side of the road. It was nearly impossible to believe that nothing was going on inside the building. It was so tall. It had such presence. I always enjoyed passing by it, feeling its presence, its suggestion of strength, the thrill of its encroachment. Now it is gone.

On the other side of the river, every week, from 1979 to

1983, photographer Mark Perrott slipped onto the demolition site of J & L's Eliza blast furnaces to create a photographic record of the closed down site. The furnaces had been a great visual symbol, welcoming the traveler along Second Avenue and the Parkway East. A classic Pittsburgh postcard shows their intricate superstructure silhouetted against the glowing downtown towers beyond. On approaching the site, Perrott has said, he felt he was entering a graveyard, and his eloquent black-and-white photographs are a heartbreaking reflection of his respect.

I am struck above all in Perrott's photographs by the quiet. And by the benevolence of the light. Life is in suspension here as idle furnaces, rain-slicked rooftops, cavernous plant sheds, a multiplicity of forms and shapes provide refuge to the ghosts of a human presence. Light falls on a shaker of salt, a coffee pot, a winch encrusted with grime. Snow mutes building lines in a wash of white. There is an uncanny stillness. But the most potent emblem of loss lies in a fallen blast furnace, its bulbous arms spilling down a slope of earth and debris to a dirt road puddled with rain. It is difficult not to feel anguish at the sight of this great hulking beast sprawled on the shattered foundation of its habitat.

"What happened in the valley is as important as what happened at Appomattox," said Randolph Harris, who grew up in Duquesne and whose entire family worked in the mill. In a sense he is right. The work of this place helped set the course of the nation. People have died here winning our wars, creating and building the world we know. The evidence of their existence remains, if only anonymously, in the buildings and bridges built with their steel. But the immediate evidence of their existence, the locus of their work, is gone. Looking out over an empty mill site, I can only wonder why it is that as a nation we are not more ready to recognize these places as hallowed ground.

"In a change of industry," Emerson wrote in *English Traits*, "whole towns are sacrificed like ant-hills, when the fashion of shoe-strings supersedes buckles, when cotton takes the place of linens, or railways of turnpikes, or when commons are enclosed by landlords." Steelworkers were not necessarily pleased as their plight became a subject of what they saw as middle-class chic. Already there had been studies, conferences, proposals from architects for remaking the valley. One proposal had suggested temporarily converting mill land at Homestead into gardens that would serve as a horticultural and agricultural exposition site. Though the idea was only part of a far larger plan, it had little attraction for people who had lost their jobs in steel. Barbara McClure, then director of the Carson Street Gallery, recalled a show of photo images presented at the gallery of the Carrie Furnaces in Rankin. A number of former steelworkers attended after seeing a write-up in the paper. Their resentment was palpable. "Where was the art community," they asked, "when we were struggling to save the mills? Does turning it into art make it all OK?"

People and Work

January 20, 8 A.M. A blanket of cloud dulls the light above the pewter gray rivers. Barges push through large platelets of ice on the surface of the Allegheny. Automobile headlights move over the bridges, as stationary lamps glow along the riverbanks and in scatters across the hillsides. Below me on the bluff deer browse in winter-dry vegetation. A pair of red-tailed hawks, scouting for prey, sweeps along the tops of the trees.

Manny Stoupis was general foreman at the blast furnaces at Duquesne from 1980 to 1984. When he arrived in June 1980, Dorothy was having trouble making twenty-eight hundred tons a day. "The place was an absolute craphouse," Manny said. By 1983 she was setting production records for a twenty-eight-foot furnace, a daily record of forty-seven hundred tons, a monthly record of over four thousand tons a day, earning blast furnace workers the U.S. Steel Ironmaster Award. "She was a real thoroughbred," Manny says, "one of the finest engineering jobs the corporation ever did by way of blast furnaces."

Manny leans back in his chair, recalling the day he closed Dorothy down. "It was really funny," he says. "She didn't want to die. We honestly said that. The last day, Monk Manns, a maintenance foreman, a little guy, was walking up the steps of the dust catcher. At the end you have to open the bells and light the gas. We didn't think there'd be much gas, but there was all kinda hydrogen there because of that wet gravel. When they opened the bells and them flares rolled off o' that hydrogen, there was an explosion like you couldn't believe. Big black cloud! Monk was so small, walking up those steps, it blew him off into the dust bin, and he come outta there, he was black, I didn't even recognize him." Manny's voice thickens with barely stifled laughter. "I said, 'Who the hell are you?' He said, 'I'm Monk, you Greek son of a bitch, you tried to kill me!'" Manny laughs, savoring the memory, then grows more serious. "You know, everybody started saying it, all the guys that were there. They said, she don't want to die. She's makin' it hard. The guys were all in love with Dorothy. There was a mystique about her. Because she was so big. Because she was unique. Because she broke records. I don't know what the hell it was. Everybody just took to her. It was like losing one of the family, I guess. Everybody believed she was alive."

Manny Stoupis is a big man, with smooth, graying dark hair slicked back from his forehead and a wide, all-embracing smile. He grew up on Jenny Lind Street in McKeesport. His father had come to this country from the island of Rhodes in 1918 or 1919, his mother from the Greek mainland in 1925. "It was the jumpiest place in the world," he says of the McKeesport of his childhood. "I ride by now, but the house ain't even there."

Manny's father worked at U.S. Steel's Christy Park Works in McKeesport, his uncle at Firth Stirling, also in McKeesport, across the river from Duquesne. Manny played football when he was young, earning athletic scholarships to the University of Pittsburgh and to Emory & Henry in Virginia. After graduating he tried out for the professional game but got cut right away and came home, finishing with the Pittsburgh Ironmen of the Atlantic Coast League. "It was only natural for me to step into the mill," he says. "That was your normal progression, just like going from first to second grade." He began as a turn foreman at the blast furnaces at E.T., on National's recommendation. He had been a laborer at National during the summers, beginning at age seventeen. "Even though I had a college degree," he said, "it was not unexpected, nor was it unbecoming, for me to become a turn foreman and to work turns. It was such a proud thing to say 'My son is a boss.'" It hurt to work Thanksgiving three to eleven, and Christmas night turns, especially when you had a family, but, he says, *it was just a way of life.* Two years after starting at E.T., he was promoted to Homestead, then from Homestead went on to National, from National to Duquesne, and in 1984 returned to E.T. "I had to laugh," he said. "It took me twenty-seven years to go full circle."

Following Manny around the blast furnace area at E.T. is a revelation. Along railroad tracks, past stockhouse bins and larry cars, over platforms and steps, watching one of the furnaces as it is tapped, he shares his thoughts, answers my questions, introduces me to each person we pass, explaining to each that I am there because I am writing a book. He lobs a mock insult at the keeper on No. 1 blast furnace, a tall, slender black man in a striped T-shirt, with hair in cornrows. The keeper grins in response. As we walk, Manny picks up a random piece of coke, an ore pellet, a chunk of Venezuelan ore and hands it to me to take home. Repeatedly, as his workers report to him, this big, voluble man calls out "I love you" in response to a favor or a job well done. I feel as though I am being introduced to a family. "You have to remember that they are people with hearts," Manny says to me, as he walks me back to my car. "Whether their I.Q. is 39 or 139, people need to be recognized."

The devaluation of working people is a commonplace in human history. It is also too easy, a failure of imagination maintained, I think, by a willful blindness to certain kinds of ability, a desire to discount what one cannot or does not want to do. Diane Novosel spoke of her brother, a pipe fitter for the city water department, as he worked on mains near the downtown Hilton. "Nobody works as hard as I do," he said, struck by the superior attitude of businessmen who passed by. A friend of mine who put himself through college working at J & L recalls the blank looks on the faces of his New York publishing colleagues when he told them he had worked in a steel mill. "I was sort of proud of it," he said. "But it meant nothing to them."

In *Fear of Falling,* Barbara Ehrenreich cites a comment about working people from a sociology text published in 1957. The working-class person, the book declares, "often fails to realize that his story is neither understandable nor interesting to the other person." I need no proof of this. I remember yet another show of photographs examining the effect of the mill closings at a gallery on the South Side. A sleekly groomed man in madras shorts leaned toward the image of a former mill worker standing in front of a line of stacks. The accompanying label read: "In the 1980s [nearly two million] manufacturing jobs were lost in the United States. . . . As manufacturing jobs have been lost, the number of retail trade and service jobs has grown. Manufacturing workers average $458 a week. The average weekly wage of retail trade workers is $204. A willingness to work is no longer enough to make ends meet or raise a family."

The man turned away from the photograph toward his companion, a well-coifed woman with frosted blond hair. "I feel so alien to all of this," he said. He shrugged, then gave the room a final cursory glance and breezed out the door.

On April 6, 1994, I was married again, to Robert Shearer, a maintenance foreman at the new continuous caster at E.T. It seems an odd alliance to some, a former editor at a New York publishing house with an apartment in Paris and a steelworker. I didn't articulate it at the time, but I have come to realize that in marrying Bob I have attached myself in yet another way to what I sense as Pittsburgh's core.

It was Bob who showed me the caster on one of my first visits to E.T. Although I had been told repeatedly that I'd never get into the mill, I finally decided I'd take a chance and write to John Goodish, the general manager, to request a tour. I mailed the letter on a Tuesday; at six the following evening he called to ask when I wanted to come.

As Bob led me through the five-story caster complex, past banks of electrical transformers and pump valves, past pipes and ducts variously colored, past roll segments and banks of computers, up and down steps, to tundish repair, to the top of the mold, to containment, to runout, where I could look back on the flowing lines of the strands, I was struck by his ease, how much he felt at home with this beautiful, complicated machine.

I was flattered, too, after a couple of hours, when his arm on the railing seemed a little too close to mine, when he allowed himself the intimacy of handing me a pretzel rather than passing me the bag. When we said good-bye, he said, "Call me." I remember thinking as I pulled out the gate, "Well, that's very sweet. But of course it's inconceivable. I'm fifty years old. I've had the love of my life. I'm writing this book. I'm happy as I am. I don't need a man in my life."

Within days I had changed my mind. I remembered the strength and feel of his handshake, his look of competence in hard hat and safety glasses, in furnace greens and metatarsal shoes. I remembered a certain innocent eagerness. I decided to hazard a phone call, to ask him to the final game of the Pirate homestand, but he wasn't there and I left a message on the machine. He didn't call me back.

And so he grew in my imagination. I wondered if he had thought it too brazen of me to call. It was the first time I'd ever asked someone out on a date. Two or three weeks went by. When he finally did call, I had more or less given up, and it was all I could do not to babble.

He took me to a tavern and eatery housed in one of the remaining nineteenth-century commercial buildings downtown and told me about growing up on a farm an hour outside of Pittsburgh, about working his way through college to earn an engineering degree, about his father who had worked in the coke fields, his seven sisters. He had never gotten my message, he said. Later in the evening, we stood side by side at one of the lookouts on Mt. Washington. The lights of the downtown buildings blazed below us, their reflections almost orange in the shimmering river. The serpentines of lighted highways extended away from us into the distant black dark. I put my hand on Bob's forearm, feeling the curve of it, the silken hair on his skin, and, conscious of the feel of flesh on flesh, let it rest there as we looked out over the city.

I see this city and its people as part of the nation's bedrock, a foundation stone on whose solid grounding the modern world is built. It is not as glossy as some others. Its values have grown out of hard, practical work. And that is what the people of the city admire: work, people who have struggled, integrity, people who try hard. They are not persuaded by hype or empty talk. I look back and think that I actually touched that soundness in the curve of Bob's arm.

Poet and steelworker Tim Russell talked to me about these values in his study one bright November afternoon. He grew up, he said, as what, in his circle and before the influence of the women's movement, was considered "a man." That is, he sired a bunch of kids and then supported them. Tim went into the mill at Weirton at the age of twenty-two and has worked there for over twenty-five years. For a long time, he says, he thought it was his responsibility to work in the mill. He had a wife and four children. It was the life he was born to. In 1980, Tim's father, three brothers, a brother-in-law, and a sister-in-law all worked at Weirton. Now there are only two. The others took early retirement or were laid off and never returned.

Now his family has "scattered to the winds." It is part of the culture of the steelworker, he says, to have family close at hand. In other times he would have been within shouting distance of his family, and at his side when his brother's child was born. He would be there for his nieces and nephews' First Communions and birthday parties. "There is something great," he says, "about sitting in an easy chair, next to your father in his easy chair, eating a plate of food, watching a bowl game on TV. It isn't the food or the game that matters, but the *extreme* bond of family. Petty disagreements are put aside. Men are in front of the firelight of the TV, women are in the kitchen comparing notes about kids. It's a good thing knowing you have that place."

I encountered the same richness of recollection in Paul Baumgartner, the son of a steelworker. Paul's father worked at J & L's South Side works for thirty years, first as a general laborer, then as an electrician's helper, as an electrician, and finally as a foreman in the No. 2 shop. "My dad always went to work," Paul says, "whether he was sick or whether he was hurt, whatever. I never *ever* remember him taking a day off." When Paul was a boy, his father would take him to Yarsky's Bar across the street from the 2 shop gate. The old-timers at the bar would tell him stories about the Coal and Iron Police. In the old days, they said, evoking an image that has become legend, if you were absent from work, the police would ride on horseback up the front steps of your house, bash the door down with the horse's hoofs, and ride into the living room to roust you out. (The Coal and Iron Police were a private company constabulary, authorized by the Pennsylvania General Assembly in 1866 and lasting into the 1930s. The force was notorious for its brutality.) Paul's father played the harmonica and had mastered a wide selection of ethnic folk songs and national anthems. If there were, say, Irish at the bar, he would launch into "Danny Boy," and the men would give Paul quarters to buy his father a beer. Paul remembers going down to the mill with his father one payday. A worker called "The Dude" stuck a gun in his father's back and growled, "Gimme yer pay." Paul didn't realize at first that it was a joke.

Paul works as a supervisor in the city's welfare department. His father considered steelworking dirty and dangerous and didn't want his son following in his footsteps. Paul is proud, though, of the strength of character he believes he developed growing up in an industrial place. "People grew up expecting to face hard situations," he said. "That was part of the deal. But along with that came opportunity. If you stuck to it and worked hard and toughed it out and put up with the rigors and dangers of the steel mill, you could make something of yourself."

I have given a good deal of thought to Pittsburgh's work ethic. It seems clear that it is not simply a version of the Protestant ethic of the city's largely Calvinist founders. There is more to it than that. The Protestant work ethic has traditionally seen work as a calling, success as a consonant of the possibility of grace. And no doubt these attitudes have been part of the mix. But, for many, work was not seen in such terms. Work was just something you did. In her article "'For Bread with Butter,'" Ewa Morawska addresses the work ethic of Eastern European immigrants. "In traditional peasant society," she writes, "work had been perceived as the attribute of human existence. It was a value in and of itself, its moral quality bearing little or no relation to its practical functions." Reinforced by the churches, the Serbian saying *covek mora da radi* (man must work) "had its exact counterpart in each and every corner of East Central Europe." Work was viewed "as part of the universal cosmic order." After serfdom was abolished and thousands of peasants began to migrate over the Continent for work and pay, "this attitude toward work was partially altered. Once the peasant discovered that work could bring money, that it brought practical, quantifiable results, it gradually began to assume a new and different meaning, entering his thinking alongside the old traditional orientation with which it was to coexist for a long time to come."

I think again of Paul Baumgartner. "The point of this place," he said, "is that this is what life is and you just do it. It's what your dad does, your neighbor does, it's just the deal. No one whined and cried."

Work didn't have to be pleasant. Diane Novosel points to

her mother's perspective. "Where did you get this notion," her mother once asked her, "that you should like what you do? Work puts food on the table, pays the bills, and you just do it. And you get down on your knees and thank God that you have it."

My husband Bob, whose mother was born of Slovak immigrants, echoes Ewa Morawska. "The ethnic work ethic derives from a desire for order," he said to me, as he drove me in his truck one afternoon along the Allegheny. "Ethnics are used to authority and they use it on themselves. They want to put it right, to have it go right, and will work hard to see it done. Work is how they support their families, and find their place within the order of things."

I ask Bob about the blue-collar definition of work.

"Blue-collar people think that if you don't want to work you get a desk job," he says. "You don't get anything done when you're sitting at a desk. You have to be doing something physical."

"So work is getting something done, accomplishing some physical task?"

"Right. They don't look at desk work as being work."

With Bob, I have begun to have a keener sense of the authenticity, the genuineness of "real work." I know that was part of his appeal for me from the beginning. He knew how to do things. He built his own house in the 1970s and added a garage soon after I met him. The idea of paying someone else to change his oil or grade his driveway is inconceivable. I have begun myself to feel a psychological distance from men "in suits," men who don't have these basic skills, though I confess I don't change my own oil.

Diane Novosel says that her background has given her a definite idea of what a man is, of the importance of being able to fix and do. She saw friends marrying guys who couldn't build a deck, couldn't fix a toilet. "It bothered me," she said of men she went out with who couldn't do these things. She says she loved when her father and her uncles worked, loved to watch men labor, was amazed at their strength and what they could do. When she was working downtown she watched the construction of a new office tower. "It was like being in the locker room where the real stuff was happening," she said. (Diane's remarks remind me of the traditional delineation of gender roles that has limited women's participation in heavy industrial work.)

What men can do. What people can do. One particular image sticks in my mind, of that night at E.T., watching Bob Mazik, the assistant strand operator at CP-3. At one point, with the ladle lowering toward the tundish, Mazik reared back toward the control panel. It was apparent that the weigh cable, which measures steel weight in the ladle, and the AMEPA cable, which measures slag level, remained unconnected. Mazik reversed the ladle's descent, moving quickly to ensure that the tundish below would not run dry of steel. I can still see him: the contrapuntal movement of outstretched arms, the feints and turns, the commingled energy of mind and body as he worked to keep those vast, dangerous elements of machinery in sync. It made me think again of a dancer, or an orchestra conductor leading the expansive, thunderous finale of a symphony.

It would be foolish, of course, to suggest that the equation of real work as physical work does not exact its price. A world that values only physical work is a world that can squelch other dreams. Pittsburgh poet Jan Beatty, who comes from a working-class background, speaks of the demon that comes to suggest to her that writing poetry is not real work. She agonizes over the fear that she is not pulling her own weight. She grew up in the atmosphere of limitation that working people themselves may unintentionally impose on their own and their children's expectations. Jan teaches at the University of Pittsburgh, but often feels, as she puts it, misplaced, like "a working-class person masquerading as a college professor." Too many jobs are seen as "not for people like us." In the culture she grew up in, jobs like teaching are regarded almost as pretend work. You go into teaching when you can't make it in the real world. Teaching is seen as being about privilege, she says, worthwhile in the sense that the pay is good, but not valued for the learning itself or the way it opens the mind. The attitudes are hard to shake.

In a review in *Pittsburgh History*, writer David Walton speaks of "the dulling and finally the defiance of the aesthetic sense," which is part of "the whole toll of mill life." This is a generalization, of course, and it has many exceptions. But, in sum, the phenomenon is undeniable. Part of it arises out of lack of exposure. But there is something else at work here and I thought I could understand it, and view it with more sympathy, one afternoon at the Carnegie Museum of Art.

I had gone to view an exhibition of photographs commemorating the centennial of the Homestead Strike, black-and-white images by Mark Perrott, Lewis Hine, Raymon Elozua, whose photographs for his "Home Scrap" project I have already described, and others. A Hew Charles Torrance landscape photographed in 1929 was a wash of grays, of factory buildings shrouded in fog and smoke. Duane Michals had posed his family before the metal shapes of the Duquesne Works, where his father, himself the son of a steelworker, had spent forty-three years of his life. Photos by W. Eugene Smith included a portrait in profile of a black steelworker, with goggles pushed up onto his forehead, the brim of his hard hat following his hair-line. A blur of lights shone in splotches in the background as the glow of the furnace highlighted the contours of his face. A trickle of sweat lined his neck. His eyes looked off into the distance, eloquent with dignity, wisdom, and a calm and re-signed realism. He had seen it all.

I wandered from the stark, white-walled room into the permanent collection nearby, toward a Renoir portrait of a young girl in a palette of pinks and browns and greens. Haunted by images of the forebearance of working men, of despair over lost jobs, the suggestion of farewell to brooding mills, I saw the silken artifice of the Renoir as thin, lacking in power and meaning. Although, deep down, I knew it was more compli-cated, I found myself wondering why it is that we exalt make-believe over the real. I understood that the workers had been grappling with powers almost larger than reason. Others had lost their place in that world. I felt the beauty in their struggle. And I understood how a more idealized form of beauty could seem irrelevant, could sometimes be pushed aside. I under-stood how the intense reality of industry could seem more sig-nificant than the transformed reality of art.

A value is placed here on what is perceived as genuine, or real. "I have no desire to become great or rich," writes B. J. Glock in an article published in the *Mill Hunk Herald*. "Doc-tors' sons become doctors, attorneys' sons become attorneys. They seem to be phonies. They understand and can relate to you one minute and don't know you or where you're coming from the next." The genuine can be a source of well-being. In his poem "The Day They Tore the Pool Room Down," steel-worker Carman Cortazzo refers to community leaders with "their respectability and their fancy dictionary talk." He won-ders what they can know

> . . . of a place where a man
> (or a boy) can go and be himself and at ease.

A heightened civility is seen as artifice, a separation of the individual from who he really is. As such it is a form of dishonesty, cloaking hidden motives, generating mistrust.

I notice in my husband Bob a fierce resistance to being subsumed by middle-class taste. It is a matter of identity, for example, not lack of education, that leads him to persist in speaking nonstandard English. To speak standard English would be to betray who he is, and, from his point of view, I think, make him less of a man. Similarly, the formulaic conventions of etiquette in letter writing or forms of greeting seem to him empty and too nice. Getting dressed up becomes a pointless and even preening self-embellishment, irrelevant to who you are and what you can do.

I saw a particularly vivid example of the power of dress to categorize one afternoon in the slab mill at E.T. An executive from U.S. Steel headquarters stepped into the operating pulpit wearing furnace greens over his suit coat and tie. I remember how out of place he seemed, how little his necktie and crisp white shirt armed him there, how they seemed to separate him from the work and the people doing it. The sight of these men seemed a telling lesson in the distance to be bridged between them. I think, too, that it is the suit's inappropriateness to real work that, in part, accounts for Bob's reluctance to wear one. A suit is not who he is.

The contrast in dress highlighted the air of capability of blue-collar workers, and reminded me of the comfort I feel in the presence of that straightforward competence. I began to wonder too at the implicit sexuality of blue-collar workers, who live so intensely in their bodies, whose T-shirts and jeans hug bodily contours, whose capability itself has sexual connotations. The suit, part of that heightened civility, hides the body. I wonder if it is this implied threat that is at least partly responsible for the disparagement of blue-collar workers.

I admit that my response to blue-collar realness is not always positive. In the constant struggle to keep the Pirates here, I feel exasperated when someone refuses to go to a ball game because of exorbitant baseball salaries. "What about football salaries?" I ask. "Well, that's different," they may say. "The Steelers earn their money," as if a willingness to hit and be hit were a more valuable commodity than grace. I grow weary of the word *fucking* when I hear it used as an adjectival hiccup. And yet I understand that rough language is both a reflection and an acknowledgement of hard, physical life. It becomes a form of swagger. As Paul Baumgartner remarked, "Wimps don't survive." It is partly this standing up to the work that gives Pittsburgh its straightforward integrity. "In Pittsburgh what you see is what you get," Paul said. "The hardness of the life would find you out so you couldn't pretend."

I would like to see this integrity as without qualification. But I know that's not very realistic. Perhaps most glaring is the fact that Pittsburgh has been no better than other cities in its treatment of African Americans. I sat with Ray Henderson one morning in the living room of his house in Forest Hills. Ray was born in Homestead, in the Ward, in 1941. At the time, his father was employed at Edgar Thomson. When I asked Ray what his father's position was, he replied that he didn't know. His father had died when he was six. Ray worked for eighteen years in the conditioning department at Duquesne, as a scarfer, then as a hand grinder, a machine grinder, a stocker, and finally as an inspector. He should have moved higher, he said, but he just got tired of the struggle. "A lot of times I came home after work and just sat on the porch trying to beat back the frustration. I didn't want to take it out on my family."

The Consent Decree of 1974, designed to provide for equal opportunity in the mill, testified to what Ray and so many others had experienced. It acknowledged that blacks (along with Hispanics and women) had been "systematically assigned to lower-paying jobs with little opportunity for advancement, denied training opportunities, and judged by more stringent qualification criteria than were White males."

A study by Abraham Epstein published in 1918 found most blacks in Pittsburgh before World War I limited to jobs as "porters, chauffeurs, janitors, and the like." Blacks who entered the city's mills and factories were for the most part confined to unskilled labor, to "the lowest rung of the economic ladder." Even through the 1930s, blacks in the iron and steel industry were used as pawns by labor *and* management. In 1875, black puddlers from Richmond and Chattanooga were brought in as strikebreakers by the Pittsburgh Bolt Company, one of many instances in western Pennsylvania in which iron and steel companies would use blacks to defeat striking workers. In 1876, three national ironworkers' unions merged to form the Amalgamated Association of Iron and Steelworkers. The organizations' whites-only policies were reversed in an attempt to discourage strikebreaking. But the admission of blacks did little to reduce the overt antagonism of white members. It is not surprising that blacks crossed picket lines even in the Homestead Strike of 1892. After the defeat of the great steel strike of 1919, a strike largely of immigrant workers in which blacks were again brought in as strikebreakers, angry white workers were heard to grumble, "The niggers did it." By 1930, blacks were deemed essential to the organization of a strong steel union. As Dennis Dickerson writes in *Out of the Crucible*, the

Steel Workers Organizing Committee pledged to represent the interests of all steel employees, regardless of skill level, and to eliminate racial discrimination both in the mills and among its own rank and file. As we have seen, the promises proved largely hollow.

I asked Ray how he accounted for the racial antagonism that has existed here. He pointed, as many do, to the fact that blacks had been used as strikebreakers, that they were perceived as having taken white men's jobs. But, he added, "a lot of people just don't feel happy unless they're standing on someone."

How are we to reconcile Pittsburgh's essential generosity with *this* failure of imagination, this sickness at the core of the American soul? I ask myself and have no answer. But the question must continue to be asked. For it is equally true that Pittsburgh is a compassionate city, loyal, patriotic, a little old-fashioned. As Jan Beatty has written, "You can count on us. . . . we'll help you change a tire, lend you a dollar, open your door, maybe even run into a burning house. When it gets down to basics, we'll be there." And, I would add, we won't make a big deal of it.

Returning to Pittsburgh has given me a clearer sense of how I came to be who I am. I understand now why I did not always feel comfortable in the glib competitiveness of New York. As an editor at Scribners, I cherished the work with the author and his manuscript, not the lunches with agents in trendy restaurants that enabled me to acquire it. It is against my instincts to make a big deal of myself. The gratification in my job was in getting into the work, into process, sinking into the manuscript and moving through the structure of its ideas.

I have heard this sense of the physicality of work articulated again and again in Pittsburgh. For eighteen years Tim

Russell worked in construction at Weirton Steel, then moved on to boiler repair. "I'm sort of a Buddhist," he says. "I think my body is supposed to do what the body is supposed to do." Tim sits tall on a chair in his study, surrounded by stacks of books and papers, in jeans and a flannel shirt, his long hair a little shaggy. I feel the force of his wide brown eyes. He mentions shoveling. "There is a lot to be said for shoveling," he says. "It exercises the body in a way that results in some accomplishment. It's not getting on a treadmill. It's real."

Jan Beatty speaks of waitressing, of "getting into the work for the work's sake," of "dissolving into the work itself." We sit across from one another at a neighborhood coffeehouse. Jan's short brown hair is capped with blond, and she is dressed in a black shirt and pants. She has held a variety of jobs—rape counselor, welfare caseworker, waitress.

"There is a value in dissolving," she says, "in getting lost in what you're doing. Even doing something as simple as filling the sugar and Sweet'N Low containers. It's not demeaning. You move from thing to thing, become your body, lose yourself as a person and become the work." Jan speaks of commitment to the work and not to its status. When people congratulate her for getting out of waitressing she replies, "What makes you think that I wanted to get out of waitressing? What makes you think [teaching] is better?"

Autoworker Doris Delaney voiced this tribute to the possibility of triumph inherent in hard, physical work in an article in the *Mill Hunk Herald*: "There is beauty in the doing of a brutal job. There's integrity in this bruised body; love between those who sweat to live; humble pride in the eyes of a worker who has defied all human limitations and proven himself stronger than those forces bent on beating him."

Others are less rhapsodic. I remember approaching a female worker, a cinder snapper, on the cast floor of one of the blast furnaces at Weirton. Her work is hard and hot, positioned as she is alongside the runners of molten iron and slag. I have heard that on cold days sweat comes off the cinder snappers as steam. Over the noise of the furnace I asked the young woman if she liked her work. "I like the money," she said.

For all his respect for physical work, Tim Russell admits that his body is "old and beat-up." Some people grow up in mill towns knowing they must do whatever they can to get away. In her *Mill Hunk* article, Doris Delaney addresses the effects of physical labor. "Hand labor is humbling," she writes. "It leaves the body bent into the shape of the job you did for however long you lasted in the foundry, factory, or mill. Certain muscles over-develop, others atrophy, the result would never fit into a designer suit."

Paul Baumgartner offers his opinion. "Factory work sucks," he says. He recalls working in a factory that used punch presses to manufacture metal shelves. "You'd get into this zone," he says, "punchin' and punchin' and punchin' and punchin'. At the end of the day, you'd have to, like, lead people away."

The rigors of blue-collar work are only compounded by management disregard. Richard Preston wrote in *American Steel* that the steel industry collapsed in part because the managers "never much cared for the men on the bottom who made the steel." Part of the success of the minimills, with their non-union work force, has been the flexibility in work rules that allows for greater productivity. At E.T. and the Irvin Works "continuous improvement" programs have been instituted which make workers part of the decision-making process on the floor and thereby tap into their practical expertise. But workers have not uniformly embraced the programs. The old distrust dies hard.

Shortly after I returned to Pittsburgh, I came across a book called *Working Classics,* an anthology of poems on industrial life, in the local interest section of a bookstore. Included in the anthology is an excerpt from *The One Song,* a long poem by C. G. Hanzlicek, in which the poet writes chillingly of how corporations can lose sight of the individual. He tells of the death of his father, a tool maker who worked in the same factory for thirty-nine years:

> The mail slot rattles,
> And with oiled fingertips
> I bring to mother
> This day's bundle of sympathy cards.
> Among them she finds
> His last check.
> Thirty-nine years,
> For Christ's sweet sake,
> And he's been docked vacation pay.
> For the one day he took
> To die on.

There is heroism here in the commitment to the work. William Serrin offers a moving tribute to the steelworkers of Homestead: "In a sense," he writes, "the workers were artists, although neither they nor almost anyone else regarded themselves so. There were electricians, carpenters, brick masons, millwrights, welders, cranemen, blacksmiths, pipe-fitters, melters, heaters, rollers, accountants, chemists, engineers, and more. They could, had they been asked, have built a city." Pittsburgh laborer and self-taught artist John Kane used the exactness he sought in a joist or a mold as a standard for the exactness he sought in his painting. I asked Tim Russell if he feels a sense of craft in his work at the mill comparable to the craft he brings to a poem. He agreed that he does. In writing a poem or fixing a machine, he says, there is the same "bringing it to rightness, when all the pieces work." (He adds that his satisfaction is greater on finishing a poem.) He mentions William Carlos Williams and his description of a poem as a well-oiled machine. "That's what a good poem does," Tim says, "sits there and hums like a good machine."

I wonder if the deep emotional bond Pittsburghers feel toward their city grows partly out of the engagement of mind and body implicit in hard work. In his essay "Are You an Environmentalist or Do You Work for a Living?" Richard White reminds us that it is through work that man became engaged with nature. Speaking of Lewis and Clark, the prototypical "first white men" in the American wilderness, White points out that "what most deeply engaged these first white men with nature, what they wrote about most vividly, was work: backbreaking, enervating, heavy work. The labor of the body revealed that nature was cold, muddy, sharp, tenacious, slippery. Many more of their adjectives also described immediate, tangible contact between the body and the nonhuman world." The journey of first white men was not "one long backpack across the West." Though aware of its beauty, they "knew and connected with the world through work." It is work, White tells us, that fully submerges us in the world. Our lives depend on it.

Part of the engagement in an industrial place comes in the operation of machines. Even today, with processes highly automated, the best operator has an instinct and finesse that set him apart. "A good operator can tell when something is starting to go bad," my husband Bob tells me, "even when everything seems to be going well. He can just feel that, say, a bearing is going, or whatever." Lawrence Kuhn wrote in his "Elegy to the Open Hearth," that "the melter or first helper who had the touch ran the furnace. Those furnace operators lacking the touch were run by the furnace." Tim Russell spoke of bringing his intuition to bear in fixing a machine, the flash of insight that allows him to set things right. Each of these examples suggests an act of the imagination akin to empathy, a projection of the self into the solidity and complexity of the industrial landscape.

"If I had it all to do again," Manny Stoupis said to me, in the living room of his house near Pittsburgh, "I'd do the same thing. I would go to the blast furnace. As bad as it's been, as hard as it was, as hot as it was. All I knew was the mills. That was the life, that was our life."

"And it grows on you," Manny's son George interjected.

"Yeah, it does," Manny said. "It does."

Paul Baumgartner believes that work, effort is the essence of life, that it is effort that creates value. "We buy everything nowadays," he says, "services, labor, oil changes. We don't know how to do things." What gives life meaning, he says, is effort, physical and mental, that you can feel. Using your body to make things happen makes life good. Changing oil makes life good. Paul has already told me that factory work sucks. And yet, he is sincere in believing, as Pittsburghers do, in physical work. "In industrial life," he says, "your senses must be in tune, everything you have is working to get the job done. You feel the sweat dribbling down your body, the heat on your brow. That's real. You know what it means to be alive."

153

The Sublime and the Beautiful

I can see the storm coming. The discrete, bread
loaf–shaped mass of gray cloud fills the Ohio River
valley to the west,
brushing and then
obliterating the hillsides
as it pushes its way toward my window. The wind
whips the trees below me on the bluff and along the
riverbanks. Whitecaps surge over the rivers' surface
and as quickly sink back into the water. The
cloudbank presses itself against my window, an
impenetrable, undifferentiated gray. Rain, whipped
by the wind, comes in slaps against the glass. The
windows swell. I move from one to another, wondering if they will hold, imagining the possible rush
of wind and water onto my furniture, my books and
papers hurtling across the room. Minutes later, the
butt of the cloudbank passes, and with it the wind

and the rain. I can see the city again, no longer

obscured by cloud. All seems quiet, suspended,

under the film of water that remains.

Paul Baumgartner sits across from me in the back room of Redbeard's, a bar on Mt. Washington's Shiloh Street. Wearing a black leather jacket, he leans against the corner of the booth, his pale brown hair falling slightly onto his forehead, his fingers resting on a bottle of Iron City beer. A mural of a mountain scene covers the wall above Paul's head. A jukebox blares and we must raise our voices to talk. Three or four young men in T-shirts and jeans throw darts just out of my line of sight.

Paul is telling me about the landscape of his childhood, about parking at night in the lot at Haines Supermarket to watch the slag dumping along Route 51. The slag is brought in by rail, in long lines of thimble cars that carry the slag in refractory-lined hemispheres. As the vessels are tipped, one and then another, a partially solidified mass of slag falls out and rolls down the hill, bouncing, with pieces breaking off, glowing red with the fire of its interior, until finally it breaks open and molten slag gushes out, lighting the hillside. "We'd sit in the car watching the pyrotechnics," Paul said. "It was like folks in the country taking you to see the waterfall."

Paul's grandfather lived on the South Side

slopes. Paul remembers sitting on the back porch, on the second floor, looking out over J & L's Pittsburgh Works. Orange and blue flames, twenty-five to thirty feet high, shot out of the stacks of the blooming mills. "The night sky and the river were lit up by these giant Roman candles," Paul says.

Paul used to take his dog to a slag dump near the Squirrel Hill Tunnel where he could run around. The hardened slag had a light, grayish cast. "It was pretty weird," he says, "acres of flat-topped crusts and wisps of scrub. It was like being on the moon."

Pittsburgh's industrial landscape was a landscape of awe, vast, surging, fiery, the epitome of what Edmund Burke and others have called the sublime. With his *A Philosophical Enquiry Into the Origin of Our Ideas of the Sublime and Beautiful*, published in 1757, Burke was largely responsible for establishing the definition of the sublime in the public mind. At its highest, Burke wrote, the sublime is a cause of astonishment, a sort of "delightful horror" arising out of the experience (from a safe distance) of terror, obscurity, difficulty, power, vastness, radiant light, "that state of the soul, in which all its motions are suspended, with some degree of horror." Lesser effects of the sublime are admiration, reverence, and respect. Beauty, on the other hand, is associated in Burke with smoothness, smallness, delicacy, a freedom from angularity. Beauty is founded on pleasure. The sublime finds its origin in the terrible and as such is productive of the strongest emotion mankind is capable of.

The idea of the sublime was easily applied, even in the eighteenth century, not only to power and grandeur in nature, to craggy peaks and vast plains, obscure chasms and violent storms, but to industrial sites. Inspired by Burke, members of the eighteenth-century British gentry, male and female, had themselves lowered in buckets into mines, toured blast furnaces, visited factories in which they marveled at the complexity and power of machines. In their published accounts we find mentions of such sights as the copper works at Llanethly, "sending up a volume of smoke . . . curling in spiral wreaths above the summits of the mountains"; the "glorious light" displayed by the smelting houses at Swansea, the "many beautiful colours from their ashes"; the machine at the silk mills at Derby "that contained 26,586 wheels making 97,746 movements." In an account of his travels published in 1780, R. J. Sullivan wrote of being lowered to the heart of a salt mine in Cheshire, "a vast glittering cavern supported by monstrous pillars which were left in the course of working the mine, colonnades forty-five feet high and eighteen feet thick supporting a roof rising to a dome."

The concept of the sublime has undergone myriad permutations since the time of Edmund Burke. But the term *sublime* remains as a means to describe the universal human emotion that arises in the face of the terrible, the feeling of awe, of astonishment or bedazzlement that, for example, I felt on first entering the BOP shop at Weirton. Putting a name on the Pittsburgh industrial landscape has been important to me. For most of my life I have heard outsiders denigrate Pittsburgh. To see the landscape as sublime somehow gives it a place. An aesthetic context. It *was* something, something else, something that we should attend to. It has a claim on our estimation that goes beyond incidental personal affection.

On my desk, in a plastic frame, I keep a snapshot of an intersection of two narrow, crumbling streets on the bluff above West Homestead. At the center of the photo a power pole rises out of a thick bank of ailanthus. Blue-and-white street signs attached to the pole barely hold their own against the vegetation encroaching from below. The signs on the pole read: Ingot Avenue and Girder Street.

In scores of neighborhoods, mills and factories were omnipresent, containing their surroundings in an eerie, inescapable embrace. Before the advent of newer steelmaking technologies and before environmental controls were in place, the fire of furnaces roofed the night with an orange/red light. Iron oxide from the open hearths cloaked houses, shrubbery, automobiles in a dull reddish dust. On windy days, black grit hit against windowpanes. At night, flecks of graphite glittered in the light of the streetlamps like snow. A cousin of mine recalls walking to school as puffs of soot brushed against his face. Senses filled with the smell of sulfur and burning coal, the pervasive taste of metal, the call of turn whistles, the booms of heavy equipment at work. Mill walls and stacks loomed all out of scale above houses clustered alongside.

"You could see the mill in the air," Paul said, "on faces and on clothing, even if you were away from it." Paul remembers as a teenager fishing for catfish in the Mon. "The river was pretty much orange in those days," he said. I asked him how he felt about that at the time. "We took it for granted," he said. "That's just the way it was."

The presence of the mills made for landscapes rife with meaning and suggestion. "Sometimes," Anna Egan Smucker wrote in *No Star Nights,* her story of growing up in a mill town in the 1950s, "we would imagine that the mill itself was a huge beast, glowing hot, breathing heavily, always hungry, always needing to be fed." One sat on the hillside looking down over the mill, gripped by subterranean booms beneath long, dark roofs and fires licking the night sky. It was a scene to inspire wonder. In the mill's voracious presence, one entered the realm of metaphor.

In his novel *The Olympian,* published in 1912, James Oppenheim portrayed the steel mill as a female body that gives birth to steel. In the steelmaking process he saw "the very birththroes of the anguished Industrial Mother. Her ingots roared in the 'wringers,' her engines shrieked and clattered in the yards, her rolls and wheels and mighty furnaces crashed and clanked and screeched." Workers, "huge and sweating laborers," were like midwives, "scorched and blinked in a glare of fire."

The industrial scene becomes explicitly sexual in "Carrie Furnace," a poem of the 1980s by poet and former steelworker Peter Blair.

> . . . To some guys it's a woman: *more nights*
> *with Carrie than the old lady.* In a steel shed
> there's a six-inch hole a worker torched
> in the wall: outside, large red lips chalked
> around it say, *Kiss me on the other side*
> where spread pink thighs surround it,
> through the hole, a view of the furnace.

Sitting at my desk, I am seized by the image of oozing, hot, annihilating metal. I visualize it in the mill, sunlike, blinding, in runners leaving the blast furnace, in ladles, in the BOP vessel. I try to open my mind to its roiling, milklike texture. A second image comes. I see myself lying flat on the mill's concrete floor, naked, arms outstretched. The business of the mill goes on around me, giant cranes, ladles, workers in hard hats. The floor feels coolly solid under my back. A sea of molten steel moves toward me over the floor, slowly, inexorably, licks at my feet. The heat washes through me as the steel climbs my shins, thighs, touches me, and my body swells to meet it with its own interior fire.

Whether the conflagration of the furnace, the bubbling

soup of molten metal, the tall, dark stacks spitting smoke or plumes of fire, the imagery of the steel mill is one of generative, erotic power. Male and female merge in its thunderous shapes and fires. There was a time when it seemed the powers of Creation itself were contained at the city's core.

To feel this link to God is the prototypical response to the sublime, and in its American, more overtly religious or "Christianized" form the sublime has been seen as a driving force in our incursions on wilderness, most pointedly in our spanning of the continent by rail. The rhetoric of this combined natural and technological sublime incorporated the belief that, as Barbara Novak writes in *Nature and Culture,* "nature and the machine would both be harnessed to the same purpose—to fulfill the American concept of a future clearly blessed by an understanding God." The impulse to the sublime remains absorbed even now into ideas of the manifest destiny of democracy and progress.

There are many who condemn the idea of progress nowadays, the idea that science and technology will lead to an ever-improving future. But I believe we cannot so easily disassociate ourselves. The landscape of Pittsburgh was a workshop. It gave the country what it wanted. It seemed there was nothing we couldn't achieve. I think of Timothy Russell's short poem, "In Nuce":

> Had you wanted apples
> the mill would not be here.
> This would still be orchard.

A friend of mine who was here on a visit remarked to me, "The history runs so deep here." I have come to realize that as I move through Pittsburgh, mentally and physically, I am carrying, living in, a story. The city is multilayered for me, so that in any view of the present I see adumbrations of what has gone before. When I drive down McArdle Roadway to the foot of Mt. Washington, I glance at the stratified, sedimentary layers of the bluff, searching for remnants of the coal that once fueled Fort Pitt. I walk along Carson Street, the South Side's main commercial street, and hear the call of a train whistle from the tracks that parallel the river. I feel the ghost of J & L and its ubiquitous industrial presence. I pass by neighborhood housefronts and stoops, or look out over rows of rooftops that fill the valleys, and think of thousands of brave, uncelebrated lives.

I am moved most of all by the human effort represented here. I sit back and look at that statement, which I have just written in longhand on the sheet of paper in front of me, and feel slightly caught out. As a daughter of Pittsburgh, I could be expected to say that. Still, when I look out over Pittsburgh, what I see is generations of people working hard to make their lives better, to care for their families, to establish themselves in a place and build a home. I see the growth of almost inconceivable industrial might—and its decline. I see the drama of the industrial landscape and the human attachments that can form to it. I see members of my own family, forging their own imaginative link to the landscape—building reservoirs and bridges, running trains. I see the difficulty of the work here and the fact that Pittsburghers were willing to do it. I think of Manny Stoupis and his assessment of the blast furnace workers at E.T. "These guys are busting their ass for their families," he said. "What could be finer than that?"

The nature writers tell us of the importance of story in providing a framework for our lives. It is the human story here, the human association with the landscape that roots me, enriches me, enlarges my sense of the engagement, the commitment that makes a good life. The story is rife with paradox and veined with darkness: the mills that gave life but also took it away; technologies that generated stupendous material wealth but poisoned the land; the smoke-filled air that meant people were working—so-called "good smoke"; the perceived invincibility of mills that nonetheless were left to die. James Wright, perhaps the most renowned of industrial poets, writes of his home, his "native country" of Martin's Ferry, Ohio, a place whose harsh realities he had long since had to leave. And yet, in his poem "Beautiful Ohio," he seizes the ambiguity of the industrial landscape and the place of the industrial landscape in the heart. The poet sits on a railroad tie above a sewer main, watching the shining waterfall of municipal refuse spilling out of the pipe into the river. The poem concludes:

> I know what we call it
> Most of the time.
> But I have my own song for it,
> And sometimes, even today,
> I call it beauty.

In one of the annotated photo-images that make up his series *I Remember Pittsburgh,* Duane Michals spoke of returning briefly to Pittsburgh in the early 1980s. "Pittsburgh is as hard and beautiful as I recall," he wrote, "like a wise and mature man, still full of his strength, but a little melancholy in his wisdom." Even now I find myself feeling startled by one aspect of that statement, the idea of Pittsburgh as a man. For me Pittsburgh, in sum, is a woman. Perhaps because of her once unsurpassed generative power, perhaps because of the emotive aura that we tend to associate with the feminine, perhaps because of the degree to which the story of the city nurtures me.

One of the criticisms of present-day Pittsburgh is that it is "inward-looking," "not progressive." I find it curious that what I perceive as the city's virtues could become its disadvantage. For the rest of the nation this city has been a place apart and we know it. We have looked to ourselves, found our sustenance within, in our families, our churches, our landscape. We are not so compelled by fashion. It seems curious to be told that in order to move into the future, we must let loose of the story that has grounded us. I think the challenge of our future is the opposite, that as we join the mainstream of coffeehouses and trendy shops and voyages through cyberspace, we must try to retain our sense of this story, a sense of who we are and what it has meant to live here.

When I travel through Pittsburgh, there is another image I carry with me, that of the painter John Kane, a man whose life and work encapsulate much of what life in the industrial landscape can mean. Kane was born in Scotland to Irish parents in August 1860 in a one-room thatched cottage with an earthen floor. His father worked mainly as a laborer during Kane's early life, digging drains and hauling away the dirt. At the age of nine, Kane began work in the shale mines of West Calder; when he was ten his father died, leaving a wife and seven children. Except for intervals in an oil works and in the coal mines, Kane continued in the shale mines, where he would be down in the pit ten to twelve hours a day. When he was nineteen, he left somewhat reluctantly for America, summoned by his stepfather, who had come in response to recruitment efforts by the Edgar Thomson Works. Scotland became a cherished memory. He was at once, in his words, "an American workman." Six feet tall with a taut, muscled frame, he "carried furnace" and worked as a top filler at Edgar Thomson, jobs that he described in his autobiography *Sky Hooks* as having "a

163

brutal effect on the men," and drew coke and sank mine shafts in the Connellsville coal region. "I did almost every kind of work a laboring man can do," he wrote. Over the course of his life he dug foundations, worked on bridge-building and other construction crews, worked as a bricklayer, as a carpenter, and in the manufacture of railroad cars; he mined coal, made one-hundred-pound shells for Westinghouse during the First World War, and painted houses, as well as offices, boxcars, and "almost the whole of an amusement park in Pittsburgh." An itinerant laborer in one of the harshest of industrial periods, he also became one of the country's foremost self-taught artists, and his paintings would find their way into museums as prominent as the Whitney and the Metropolitan Museum of Art. Sky hooks are "the curves of steel from which a house painter hangs his scaffold." Kane called his autobiography *Sky Hooks* at the suggestion of Marie McSwigan, the reporter for the *Pittsburgh Press* who acted as co-author, because, she said, "the tools of his lowly trade had been instruments with which to reach the stars."

Kane's life was not without sorrow. In 1904, on the day after he was born, Kane's infant son died. Kane plunged into depression, drinking heavily, and leaving home for extended periods of time. After his wife finally left him, taking their two daughters with her, he joined his family only for brief intervals over a period of twenty-five years.

Still, as the years passed, there was the work. Kane had sketched as a child and learned to mix colors by painting freight cars. During his lunch breaks he would draw "scenes" on the sides of boxcars, then color them before painting over them once the lunch break was finished. Sometime before 1910, he sold his first painting, a landscape of the farm owned by a family named Steel. He sold the painting to "young Mr. Steel" for a price of twenty-five dollars. He had been on the point of approaching the house with the painting when he noticed that he had left out a small bay window. A week later, having added the window and the vines growing beneath it, he returned to the house. "Hasn't he got the bay window fine!" the ladies exclaimed. Attention to detail would remain a hallmark of Kane's work.

John Kane is one of the preeminent interpreters of the industrial landscape. In scenes of Pittsburgh's hills and rivers, its bridges, clustered houses, railroads, steel mills, and smoking stacks, lines and arcs of the natural and the man-made come together to reflect the design of an ordered universe in which industrial man is at home. They are scenes imbued with empathy, with a gentleness and an innocence that belie the apparent difficulties of his life. "Truth is love in thought," Kane wrote. "Beauty is love in expression. Art and painting are both of these."

Scene in the Scottish Highlands was the first of Kane's paintings to be accepted for the Carnegie Institute International (it was accepted for the exhibition of 1927), and the first to bring him a measure of fame. Kane was living alone and out of touch in the Strip District when the letter from the Carnegie arrived. By himself in his tenement room, and longing for some sort of celebration, he pulled out a tin whistle and played a Highland fling for the little girls in the painting to dance to. "It was my way," he said, "of communicating the good news." A month after the show opened Kane's wife returned.

John Kane died on August 10, 1934, of tuberculosis, in the Tuberculosis League Hospital. He had spent much of his life recording the "snatches of beauty" he saw around him. He was buried in Calvary Cemetery, attended by a small group of mourners, in the rain, after a life of physical and imaginative engagement with a place. "I have been asked why I am particularly interested in painting Pittsburgh," he wrote in his autobiography, "her mills with their plumes of smoke, her high hills and deep valleys and winding rivers. Because I find beauty everywhere in Pittsburgh. It is the beauty of the past which the present has not touched. The city is my own. I have worked on all parts of it, in building the blast furnaces and then in the mills and in paving the tracks that brought the first street cars out Fifth Avenue to Oakland. The filtration plant, the bridges that span the river, all these are my own."

Notes

This section is intended to point the reader to sources for which sufficient information does not already appear in the text.

Prologue

Willard Glazier, *Peculiarities of American Cities* (Philadelphia, 1883), as excerpted in *Pittsburgh*, ed. Roy Lubove (New York, 1976).

"touched by Pittsburgh": David Lewis in *Remaking Cities: Proceedings of the 1988 International Conference in Pittsburgh* (Pittsburgh, 1989).

"forty major industrial plants closed": All but the final statistic comes from "Does Making Things Matter?," produced by WQED/Pittsburgh in association with the Carden Company, 1994.

Out of This Land

For the section on the area's prehistory, I am indebted to the Benedum Hall of Geology at the Carnegie Museum of Natural History and to Albert Kollar, collection manager in the museum's Department of Invertebrate Paleontology.

The quotes from James Kenny, John May, the French traveler (J.C.B.), David McClure, Mrs. Mary Dewees, John Melish, David Thomas, John Pearson, and Russell Errett, along with indications of original sources, appear in *Crossroads: Descriptions of Western Pennsylvania, 1720–1829*, ed. John W. Harpster (Pittsburgh, 1938).

John Heckewelder, *The Travels of John Heckewelder in Frontier America*, ed. Paul A. W. Wallace (Pittsburgh, 1958).

Nicholas Cresswell, *The Journal of Nicholas Cresswell, 1774–1777* (New York, 1924).

Christian Schultz Jr., *Travels on an Inland Voyage* (New York, 1810).

For the historical overview on pages 20–28, I am indebted to Solon J. Buck and Elizabeth Hawthorn Buck, *The Planting of Civilization in Western Pennsylvania* (Pittsburgh, 1939; rpt. 1967); Leland D. Baldwin, *Pittsburgh: The Story of a City, 1750–1865* (Pittsburgh, 1937); Stephan Lorant, *Pittsburgh: The Story of an American City* (New York, 1964); and Robert C. Alberts, *The Shaping of the Point: Pittsburgh's Renaissance Park* (Pittsburgh, 1980).

Joshua Gilpin, *Pleasure and Business in Western Pennsylvania, The Journal of Joshua Gilpin, 1809,* ed. Joseph E. Walker (Harrisburg, 1975).

The lists of products on pages 28 and 29 are from Catherine Elizabeth Reiser, *Pittsburgh's Commercial Development, 1800–1850* (Harrisburg, 1951).

The information on Pittsburgh's first steam-powered mills and factories is from Buck and Buck, *The Planting of Civilization in Western Pennsylvania.*

John Bernard, *Retrospectives of America, 1797–1811* (New York, 1887), as quoted in Rina C. Youngner, "Paintings and Graphic Images of Industry in Nineteenth Century Pittsburgh: A Study of the Relationship Between Art and Industry," Ph.D. dissertation, University of Pittsburgh, 1991.

Anthony Trollope, *North America* (New York, 1862).

James Parton, "Pittsburg," *Atlantic Monthly,* January 21, 1868, as excerpted in Lubove, *Pittsburgh.*

For the keelboat, the keelboatmen, and the rise of steam, see Leland D. Baldwin, *The Keelboat Age on Western Waters* (Pittsburgh, 1941; rpt. 1969); Lee Gutkind, *The People of Penn's Woods West* (Pittsburgh, 1984); Walter Kidney, *The Three Rivers* (Pittsburgh, 1982); and Annie Dillard, "River Goods," *Pittsburgh History* (Winter 1994–1995). The quotes from Mike Fink are from Kidney.

VESSELS OF FIRE

James J. Davis, *The Iron Puddler: My Life in the Rolling Mills and What Came of It* (Indianapolis, 1922).

I learned of the Slovak expression *za chlebom* in Paul Krause, *The Battle for Homestead, 1880–1892* (Pittsburgh, 1992).

For the material on Carnegie and Frick, I am indebted to Joseph

Frazier Wall, *Andrew Carnegie,* 2nd ed. (Pittsburgh, 1989), and Paul Krause, *The Battle for Homestead.* Also useful is the section on Andrew Carnegie in Roy Lubove, "Pittsburgh and the Uses of Social Welfare History," in *City at the Point: Essays on the Social History of Pittsburgh,* ed. Samuel P. Hays (Pittsburgh, 1989).

For the material on the Homestead Strike and the steel industry at that time, I am indebted to Arthur G. Burgoyne, *The Homestead Strike of 1892* (1893; Pittsburgh, 1979); Paul Krause, *The Battle for Homestead; "The River Ran Red": Homestead 1892,* ed. David P. Demarest Jr. (Pittsburgh, 1992); and Tim Ziaukas, "Lockout!" *Pittsburgh Magazine* (June 1992).

Irwin Shapiro's version of the Joe Magarac story is *Joe Magarac and His U.S.A. Citizen Papers* (1962; rpt. Pittsburgh, 1979). Joe's diet of "hot steel soup" and "old ingots for meat" is from a song written in 1946 by Jacob A. Evanson, which appears in George Swetnam, *Pittsylvania Country* (1951; rpt. Greensburg, Pa., 1992).

For a more thorough look at the debate over Joe Magarac's origins, see George Carver, "Legend in Steel," *Western Pennsylvania Historical Magazine* 27 (September–December 1944); Peter Oresick, "Joe Magarac: The Manufacturing of an American Folk Hero," unpublished paper, Library and Archives Division, Historical Society of Western Pennsylvania, Pittsburgh, Pa., 1980; Hyman Richman, "The Saga of Joe Magarac," *New York Folklore Quarterly,* 9, no. 4 (Winter 1953); Roy Kahn, "Just an Average Joe," *Pittsburgh Magazine* (November 1985).

John A. Fitch, *The Steel Workers* (1910; rpt. Pittsburgh, 1989), and Crystal Eastman, *Work-Accidents and the Law* (1910; rpt. New York, 1969), are the Pittsburgh Survey volumes referred to.

THE CONTOURS OF HOME

The statistics on the substructure of the Fort Duquesne Bridge are from "Substructure in for Pittsburgh Bridge," *Constructioneer,* October 12, 1959.

"Home is land": Janet R. Horsch, "Gott Ist die Liebe / Er Liebt auch Mich," *Creative Nonfiction,* no. 3 (1995).

Corinne Azen Krause, *Grandmothers, Mothers, and Daughters: Oral Histories of Three Generations of Ethnic American Women* (Boston, 1991).

For the Filaret Society and the history of Immaculate Heart of

Mary Church, see the pamphlet honoring the church's Diamond Jubilee in 1972. A copy can be found in the Library and Archives Division of the Historical Society of Western Pennsylvania, Pittsburgh, Pa.

Frances Babic of the Croatian History Museum in Eastlake, Ohio, pointed out the practice of Slavic women to mourn in community, as well as the similarity of the women's dress to that of the transept Virgins and the Byzantine posture of the central Madonna, in a lecture at Saint Nicholas Millvale, April 1995.

Michael Novak, "Confessions of a White Ethnic," in *White Ethnics: Their Life in Working Class America,* ed. Joseph Ryan (Englewood Cliffs, N.J., 1973).

THE LOSS OF THE MILLS

The videotape from the Historical Society of Western Pennsylvania is called "Life Below the Tracks," from the exhibit "Homestead: The Story of a Steeltown" (1989).

Saint Mary Magdalene Church: "Mon Valley Saves Beloved Church," *Pittsburgh Post-Gazette,* December 9, 1996.

Carnegie's remarks at the dedication of the Carnegie Library of Homestead are quoted in William Serrin, *Homestead: The Glory and Tragedy of an American Steel Town* (New York, 1992).

The material on the dismantling and cataloging of the 48-inch mill is from a videotape called "Preservation of the 48" Mill," produced in 1991 by the Steel Industry Heritage Task Force, Homestead, Pa.

Patricia Dobler, "Steelmark Day Parade, 1961," *Talking to Strangers* (Madison, 1986).

Peter Blair, "Iron Heritage and Steel Dreams," *In Pittsburgh Newsweekly,* October 20–26, 1994.

Tom Dawson, "Artist's Work Forges New Appreciation of Steelworkers," *Pittsburgh Press,* August 4, 1988.

For the discussion of the decline of Big Steel, the DMS, and the Save Dorothy campaign, I am indebted to John P. Hoerr, *And the Wolf Finally Came: The Decline of the American Steel Industry* (Pittsburgh, 1988); William Serrin, *Homestead;* James B. Burnham, *Changes and Challenges: The Transformation of the U.S. Steel Industry,* Center for the Study of American Business, Policy Study Number 115, March 1993; and Dale A. Hathaway, *Can Workers Have a*

Voice? The Politics of Deindustrialization in Pittsburgh (University Park, Pa., 1993).

The Locker quote is from Hathaway, *Can Workers Have a Voice?*

Wesley R. Slusher's diary/scrapbook, "My Time at U.S. Steel, Duquesne Works, Duquesne, Penna.," is in the collection of the Historical Society of Western Pennsylvania, Library and Archives Division, Pittsburgh, Pa.

The material on Bob Macey is from "Shutdown Prompts Memories," *Daily News* (McKeesport, Pa.), May 25, 1984.

The originals of the steelworkers' letters were reproduced in a pamphlet entitled *Chicago Steelworkers: The Cost of Unemployment*, Steelworkers Research Project, by Julie S. Putterman, project director, sponsored by Hull House Association and Local 65 United Steelworkers of America, January 1985.

David Walton, review of William Serrin's *Homestead* and *"The River Ran Red,"* ed. David P. Demarest Jr., in *Pittsburgh History* (Fall 1993).

The material on Ken Johnston is from "Jobless Adrift, Cling to Hope," by Jane Blotzer, *Pittsburgh Post-Gazette*, December 30, 1985.

Perrott's Eliza series has been published as *Eliza: Remembering a Pittsburgh Steel Mill*, photographs by Mark Perrott, introduction by John R. Lane (Charlottesville, Va., 1989).

PEOPLE AND WORK

Ewa Morawska, "'For Bread with Butter': Life-Worlds of Peasant-Immigrants from East Central Europe, 1880–1914," *Journal of Social History* (Spring 1984).

David Walton, review of *Homestead* and *"The River Ran Red."*

Jan Beatty, "a working-class person masquerading as a college professor": from an interview in *In Pittsburgh Newsweekly*, December 14–20, 1995.

B. J. Glock's "Interview of a Worker" and Carman Cortazzo's "The Day They Tore the Pool Room Down" can be found in *Overtime: Punchin' Out with* The Mill Hunk Herald *Magazine (1979–1989)* (Pittsburgh and Albuquerque, 1990).

Abraham Epstein, *The Negro Migrant in Pittsburgh*, University of Pittsburgh, School of Economics, 1918, as excerpted in Lubove, *Pittsburgh*.

For the historical material on African-American steelworkers, I

171

am indebted to Dennis C. Dickerson, *Out of the Crucible: Black Steelworkers in Western Pennsylvania, 1875–1980* (Albany, N.Y., 1986).

Jan Beatty, "My Pittsburgh," introduction to *Pittsburgh Revealed* (catalogue for photo exhibit) (Carnegie Museum of Art, 1997). The quoted phrases, "getting into the work for the work's sake," "dissolving into the work itself," and the questions beginning "What makes you think . . . ?" are from *In Pittsburgh Newsweekly,* December 14–20, 1995.

Doris Delaney's "Burnt Peas" can be found in *Overtime.*

Working Classics: Poems on Industrial Life, ed. Peter Oresick and Nicholas Coles (Urbana and Chicago, 1990).

Richard White, "Are You an Environmentalist or Do You Work for a Living?: Work and Nature," in *Uncommon Ground: Toward Reinventing Nature,* ed. William Cronon (New York, 1995).

Lawrence Kuhn, "Elegy to the Open Hearth," *Magazine of Metals Producing* (December 1969).

The Sublime and the Beautiful

The quotes on eighteenth-century industrial sites are from Esther Moir, "The Industrial Revolution: A Romantic View," *History Today* 9 (1959).

James Oppenheim, quoted in David E. Nye, *The American Technological Sublime* (Cambridge, Mass., 1994).

Peter Blair, "Carrie Furnace," *A Round, Fair Distance from the Furnace* (Fox River Grove, Ill., 1993).

Timothy Russell, "In Nuce," *Adversaria* (Evanston, Ill., 1993).

James Wright, "Beautiful Ohio," *Above the River: The Complete Poems* (New York and Hanover, N.H., 1990).

For the discussion of John Kane, I am indebted to *John Kane, Painter,* compiled by Leon Anthony Arkus (Pittsburgh, 1971), which contains a reprint of Kane's autobiography *Sky Hooks,* as told to Marie McSwigan, and a foreword and catalogue raisonné of Kane's paintings by Arkus.

Acknowledgments

Above all, I would like to salute the people of southwestern Pennsylvania, whose kindness and generosity have made this book possible. At every turn, people gave me their time, remained patient with my questions, and eagerly suggested leads to information I might need. Many who helped me are mentioned in the text, some are not. I would like to thank everyone who helped me by name.

At U.S. Steel: John Goodish, Bob Harris, Keith Howell, Ken Matsko, Bob Maxson, Bob Mazik, Bob Shearer, Manny Stoupis, and Shirley Zafris. At Weirton Steel: Ralph Cox, Harry Jarvis, Dick Kimmel, and Glenn McIntyre. At Braeburn Steel: Brad Huwar and Rich Verner. All were extremely helpful in explaining the process of making steel.

In Polish Hill: Wanda Antoszewski, Frances Catania, Toni Dobies, Harry Harenski, Richard Michalowski, Gertrude Philips, Vicki Pleczkowski, Chris Potochnik, Jane Radziewicz, Father Joe Swierczynski, Helen and Sharon Wolkiewicz, and Richard and Millie Zielmanski. All were especially generous in allowing me to intrude into their lives.

Poets Jan Beatty, Pat Dobler, and Tim Russell provided invaluable insights into the meaning of work, as did Paul Baumgartner, who also made vivid for me the industrial landscape of his childhood.

Diane Novosel talked to me at length about her family story, and Leonard Fleming and Frank Stanford generously shared their memories of the Homestead Works. My father- and mother-in-law, Bud and Sue Shearer, told me about work at the coke ovens. Ray Henderson spoke eloquently about the trials and the courage of African Americans here. Randy Harris and Joel Sabadasz helped to get me started by pointing me to the people I needed to know. Albert Kollar at the Carnegie Museum of Natural History read the section on the area's prehistory; Fran Babic of the Croatian History Museum

173

in Eastlake, Ohio, read the section on the Saint Nicholas murals. Dave Demarest, Lee Gutkind, and Peter Oresick made helpful comments on the manuscript. Reidar Bjorhovde, Mark Brown, Doris Dyen, Bill Gaughan, Russ Gibbons, Ellen Kight, Vicki Leonelli, Joel Sabadasz, and Dina Vargo helped me to chase down or verify details. Doe Coover, a native Chicagoan, offered her enthusiasm and her understanding of industrial places. I am indebted to them all. I also wish to salute the collections and staff of the Carnegie Library of Pittsburgh, the Hillman Library and the Darlington Collection at the University of Pittsburgh, and the Library and Archives Division of the Historical Society of Western Pennsylvania. Thanks too to Cynthia Miller and her colleagues at the University of Pittsburgh Press, who handled my book with utmost professionalism and care.

Finally, I want to thank my husband Bob Shearer, who never once complained as the book threatened to take over our lives.

⚜

Grateful acknowledgment is made to quote from the following copyrighted material: "Carrie Furnace," from *A Round Fair Distance from the Furnace*, by Peter Blair, copyright © 1993 Peter Blair, reprinted by permission of Peter Blair and White Eagle Coffee Store Press; "The Day They Tore the Pool Room Down," by Carman Cortazzo, from *Overtime: Punchin' Out with* The Mill Hunk Herald *Magazine (1979–1989)*, published by West End Press in cooperation with Piece of the Hunk Publishers, Inc. in 1990, copyright © 1990 Piece of the Hunk Publishers, Inc., reprinted by permission of West End Press. *Overtime* is available from West End Press; "Steelmark Day Parade, 1961," from *Talking to Strangers*, by Patricia Dobler, copyright © 1986, reprinted by permission of the University of Wisconsin Press; "The One Song," from *Calling the Dead*, by C. G. Hanzlicek, copyright © 1982 C. G. Hanzlicek, reprinted by permission of Carnegie Mellon University Press; *I Remember Pittsburgh*, 1982, by Duane Michals, American b. 1932, gelatin silver print sequence, nine photographs, each image 8 x 10 in. (20.32 x 25.40 cm), Carnegie Museum of Art, Pittsburgh; Greenwald Photograph Fund and Fine Art Discretionary Fund, 83.10.1-9, by permission of Duane Michals and the Carnegie Museum of Art; "In Nuce," from *Adversaria*, by Timothy Russell, copyright © 1993 Timothy Russell, published by TriQuarterly Books/Northwestern University Press in 1993. All rights reserved; reprinted by permission of Northwestern University Press.

Index

facilities of, 41, 102, 117; Manny Stoupis at, 133–35; workers at, 58, 118, 150
Ehrenreich, Barbara, 135
Electricity, 8
"Elegy to the Open Hearth" (Kuhn), 152–53
Eliza blast furnaces, 130
Elozua, Raymon, 127
Emigration, 9, 109
English, vs. French, 6, 22–26
English Traits (Emerson), 131
Epstein, Abraham, 147
Errett, Russell, 31
Europe, 118
Evans, George, 29–30
Experimental Negotiating Agreement (ENA), 118

Families, 138; in immigrant experience, 84, 88, 100; in industrial landscapes, 69–72; in steel mills, 115, 161
Fear of Falling (Ehrenreich), 135
Ferris, Peter, 66
Fink, Mike, 32–33
Fish, plentitude of, 19–20
Fitch, John, 63
Fleming, Leonard, 109, 112, 115–16
Forbes, Brigadier General John, 25–26
Forests, of Allegheny Mountains, 19–20
Forks of the Ohio, the, 22–23; forts on, 23–27. *See also* Point, the
Fort Duquesne, 6, 24–26
Fort Duquesne Bridge, 68–69
Fort Le Boeuf, 23
Fort Pitt, 6, 26–27
Fort Prince George, 23–24
Forts, English and French, 6, 22–24, 26–27
48" Universal Mill (panel by Qualters), 111
Frazier, John, 21–22

French, 6, 21; vs. English, 22–26
French and Indian War, 24
Frick, Henry Clay, 8; and Carnegie, 51–53, 55–56; coke production by, 54–55; strikebreaking by, 58–61
Frontier, 27, 32
Fulton, Robert, 33
Funiculars (inclines), 7
Furnaces, 15, 64; basic oxygen, 36–37, 43, 116–17; batch reheat, 47; open hearth, 44, 57. *See also* Blast furnaces; Open hearth furnaces

Garland, M. M., 60
Gas, 18
Gender, 162
Geography, 15–16
Geology, 15–17
Gilpin, Joshua, 29
Gist, Christopher, 22
Glass, 29
Glazier, Willard, 7
Glock, B. J., 144
Goodish, John, 136
Government, 60, 62
Graham, Albert, 70–71
Graham, Charles, 71
Grant, Major James, 25
Gropper, William, 63

Hall, Charles Martin, 8
Hanzlicek, C. G., 151
Harenski, Harry, 78–80
Harris, Randolph, 115, 130
Heckewelder, John, 19
Henderson, Ray, 146–48
Hewitt, Abram, 68
Hine, Lewis, 44
Historic American Engineering Record (HAER), 103, 112
Historical Society of Western Pennsylvania, 105
Hoerr, John, 121